The Four-Season Vegetable Gardener's Bible [9 in 1]

From Seed to Harvest - Your Updated and Trusted Guide to Cultivating Your Green Thumb and Enjoying Freshness Throughout the Seasons

Mildred Jobbins

Copyright © 2023 by Mildred Jobbins

All rights reserved. No part of this publication may be reproduced, distributed, or transmitted in any form or by any means, including photocopying, recording, or other electronic or mechanical methods, without the prior written permission of the publisher, except in the case of brief quotations embodied in critical reviews and certain other noncommercial uses permitted by copyright law.

Table of Contents

Book 1 - Selecting the Best Vegetables for Year-Round Growing 5

   Prioritizing hardy, resilient varieties 5

   Choosing early, mid season, and late producers 7

   Matching plants to your climate conditions 9

   Recommended crops for each season 13

Book 2 - Using Structures to Extend the Growing Season 18

   Cold frames, hoop houses and greenhouses 18

   Heating and ventilation systems 20

   Installing shade structures 21

   Frost protection strategies 23

Book 3 - Building Fertile Soil for Optimal Plant Health 25

   The importance of organic matter and compost 25

   Testing and amending soil pH and nutrients 27

   Fertilization needs by season 28

   Cover crops and green manures 30

Book 4 - Watering Methods for Efficient Irrigation 33

   Drip irrigation, soaker hoses, and sprinklers 33

   Setting up rainwater collection systems 34

   Techniques for reducing water usage 36

   Mulching to retain moisture 37

Book 5 - Pest Prevention and Organic Solutions 42

   Identifying common garden pests 42

   Organic and natural control options 43

   Companion planting strategies 46

   Preventive measures like row covers 48

Book 6 - Seed Starting and Propagation for Ongoing Harvests 51

   Grow lights, heating mats and trays 51

   Timing seed starts for continuous yields 55

   Hardening off and transplanting methods 57

   Saving seeds from your best plants 60

Book 7 - Designing Your Layout for Year-Round Production 62

   Arranging for crop rotation 62

Maximizing sun throughout the seasons 64

Strategies for small spaces 66

Incorporating vertical growing.. 68

Book 8 - Maintaining Optimal Growing Conditions 70

Temperature, light and ventilation management.. 70

Caring for plants in extreme weather 72

Trellising, staking and pruning over time 74

Ensuring excellent flavor and nutrients... 76

Book 9 - Preserving and Storing Your Harvest Bounty 78

Freezing, canning, drying and cold storage 78

Fermenting and pickling 80

Preventing waste of surplus produce... 83

Selling or donating extras.. 85

Bonus Book 1 - Getting Started with Hydroponics 87

Overview of hydroponic gardening methods... 87

Selecting an indoor or outdoor hydroponic system..................................... 89

Choosing the right hydroponic growing media 90

Maintaining optimal nutrient levels 92

Bonus Book 2 - Leveraging Vertical Space for Increased Yields 95

Benefits of vertical gardening.. 95

Types of vertical structures and supports.. 96

Training vining crops to climb vertically 98

Optimizing sunlight for vertical crops 100

Bonus Book 3 - Embracing Permaculture Principles for Sustainable Gardening .103

Introduction to Permaculture 103

Designing a Permaculture Garden Here 104

Permaculture Techniques for Year-Round Gardening...................................106

Book 1 - Selecting the Best Vegetables for Year-Round Growing

Prioritizing hardy, resilient varieties

The key to achievement lies in making smart choices about variety. These characteristics, I've observed, guarantee financial success no matter the vagaries of the seasons:

Resistance to disease is given the highest priority because fungal problems might be catastrophic without resistant genetics. While other varieties of beet lose their productivity due to leaf spot, 'Releaser' beet continues to thrive. Despite the vulnerability that generally inhibits members of the Brassicaceae family, brassicas like 'Decimus' kale are thriving.

The ability to tolerate cold lengthens the growing season. The 'Ambassador' cabbage is more resistant to frost damage than other varieties. When other alternatives are limited, 'Bloomsdale' spinach and 'Carillon' radish relish cool well while still providing essential nutrients. Heat resistance proves to be equally important, like the capacity of "Genovese" basil to season meals all throughout the summer.

The confined areas that are typical of intense production are ideal for the growth of compact habits. Bush beans such as 'Provider' produce a heavy harvest without spreading too much. Dwarf cucumbers produce a large harvest while having a little footprint.

Short-season varieties can be planted in between longer-term crops to maintain a continual harvest. The 'Galactic' variety of lettuce develops quickly, allowing for several harvests. The 'Early Girl' tomato yields fruit both early and late, increasing the length of time during which ripe orbs may be harvested.

A consistent rate of germination guarantees an acceptable number of starts within constrained time constraints. Packets that advertise crimped cotyledons use up valuable room inside that may be better utilized by proven performers.

In the past, as part of an experiment, I grew only open-pollinated heirlooms, but the weather ended up destroying my efforts. Refining the features that drive dependable harvests in spite of unpredictability has reignited my enthusiasm and motivates year-round celebrations. When expectations aren't met by reality, selection's significance becomes abundantly evident. When intuition is developed, success is sure to follow.

When selecting hardy vegetable types, the following are some extra considerations to take into account:

- Resistance to diseases and pests: Search for genes that provide protection against common afflictions such as late blight in tomatoes, mildew in greens, or beetle damage in brassicas.

- Select cultivars that have been developed specifically for your growing zone in order to adapt to the changing climate. Gardens in the south are ideal for heat-resistant varieties, while gardens in the north are best suited for cold-resistant varieties.

- The adaptability of the soil: Some plants, such as radishes and carrots, can dependably yield fruit in a variety of soil conditions. Some plants can't reach their full potential without having their soil adjusted.

- Low water requirements: plants that can withstand dry spells, such as thyme, kale, and Swiss chard, are able to store moisture and maintain their quality despite the lack of water.

Extended harvest windows: Varieties that yield fruit over an extended period of time increase agricultural output. Contrary to early-bolting determinates, cherry tomatoes continue to set fruit throughout the season.

- Higher levels of vitamins, minerals, and antioxidants than those found in conventional cultivars are found in varieties that have undergone nutritional enhancement.

- Ripening at the same rate throughout: timely harvesting is made possible by crops that mature at the same rate, preventing losses due to rot or pests.

- Longevity in storage: Varieties that maintain their quality for longer after harvest result in less wasted food and more availability.

Obtaining these hardy characteristics may be rewarding for novice and experienced gardeners equally if done with sufficient knowledge, gardening lore, and regional experience.

Choosing early, mid season, and late producers

A garden that has been carefully managed may give fresh vegetables for virtually the whole year. Selecting a range of plants with varying maturation dates is the key to reaching this goal, since this method is both straightforward and fruitful in its execution. This strategy guarantees a steady supply of veggies throughout the year by sourcing them from early growers in the spring, mid-season producers in the summer, late producers in the fall, and even winter growers.

Acquiring Knowledge about the Maturity of Plants
Every type of plant has its own unique development schedule, which is measured in "days to maturity." This is the average number of days it takes for a plant to reach the stage when it is ready to be harvested after it has been planted (or transplanted) in the ground. Gardeners can better prepare for a consistent supply of food throughout the year if they have a solid knowledge of this notion.

The Original Creators
Vegetables that are picked during the early part of the growing season are the first to reach full maturity and can be eaten. These plants are mostly those that produce vegetables during the chilly season, or those that do well in temperatures that are lower and are hardy enough to survive a little frost. Radishes, lettuces, spinach, peas, and broccoli are some examples of such vegetables. The average time required for these plants to reach maturity is between 30 and 60 days.

Consider varieties that claim the word "early" in their names or descriptions while making your choice among early growers. These are frequently bred for the express purpose of increasing their rate of maturation. Planting early-maturing crops in stages over a period of several weeks can allow you to extend the harvesting season.

Producers for the Midpoint of the Season
Mid-season producers are generally warm-season veggies, which means that they thrive throughout the warmer summer months. These plants, which can take anywhere from sixty to ninety days to reach maturity, include tomatoes, cucumbers, zucchini, peppers, and maize. After the threat of frost has gone and the soil temperature has sufficiently increased, they are planted.
Consider planting your crops in succession so that you may get the most out of your mid-season harvest. This entails sowing new seeds approximately once every two to three weeks, which will provide a constant yield throughout the whole growing season.

Late Composers and Producers
Late-season producers are plants that take the longest to develop and can be harvested as late as the fall or even the winter. Late-season producers take the longest to mature. Vegetables such as Brussels sprouts, parsnips, pumpkins, winter squashes, and certain varieties of kale are included in this category. These plants have a maturation period that is frequently longer than ninety days, are able to resist lower temperatures, and in certain circumstances, their flavor improves after being exposed to frost.

In addition to these groups of vegetables, there are others, such as kale, Swiss chard, and carrots, that may be produced virtually continuously throughout the year in areas that are warmer. These adaptable plants are able to bridge the harvesting gap between early, mid, and late in the season.

Creating a Plan for Your Garden
Planning is very necessary in order to properly implement this strategy. Make a rough drawing of your garden, noting where and when you will plant each type of vegetable, and then draw the sketch. Take into account the individual requirements that each plant has,

such as its preferred amount of sunshine, amount of space, and companion plants.

It is important to rotate your crops on a yearly basis in order to minimize the buildup of diseases and pests and to preserve the fertility of the soil. Crop rotation is an age-old strategy that has not only been shown to be excellent for the overall health of the garden, but also enables more effective utilization of space during the course of the year.

The Advantages of Having a Wide Selection

There are a lot of advantages to cultivating several kinds of plants, each of which reaches maturity at a different period. It makes the most efficient use of the area in your garden, it lengthens the harvesting season, and it may supply a wide variety of nutrients derived from the many crops that are gathered. Additionally, it enriches the aesthetic attractiveness of your garden by contributing a vivid combination of colors and textures to the overall design of the space.

When you embark on the exciting world of gardening all year round, it is important to keep in mind that patience and adaptability are your allies. It's acceptable if not all of your vegetables grow exactly like you hoped they would. Learning from each experience, adjusting your strategy as necessary, and taking pleasure in the process are all essential components of what makes gardening such a rewarding hobby. You are not merely growing a garden when you select a combination of early, mid-season, and late-season producers; rather, you are nurturing a year-round food factory that will reward you with improved health, a greater sense of fulfillment, and a more profound connection to the natural world.

Matching plants to your climate conditions

The key to successful crop production is not only picking the right types but also combining them in ways that are optimal. It is impossible for the people who live in a garden to be disappointed since their surroundings are so well suited to them. Before I learned about compatibility keys, my weather circumstances caused a number of issues. I now chose mates who are married for the sake of prosperity using the intuition that I learned from both triumphs and disappointments.

By gaining an awareness of the distinguishing characteristics of my growth zone, appropriate partners presented themselves. The length of the season, the quantity of rainfall, the temperature extremes, and the humidity levels all have an impact on one's health. Microclimates within the building, such as reflected heat from surfaces, provide residents alternatives that their neighbors do not have. Investigating previously untapped areas opened up a broader range of opportunities than was initially apparent.

Ratings of hardiness reflect the cold endurance of different varieties, which is helpful for strategy. Half-zones are transitory places that need reassessment of one's goals and expectations. Again, microclimates allow solutions, such as the sun warming a plot over the indicated heat units when it is funneled via a canyon. Through creative thinking that goes beyond the norm and keen observation, boundaries point out but do not confine.

The staggered delivery of crops that result from succession planting fulfills appetites throughout the year. Along with plants that are chemically effective in warding off temperature-sensitive pests, cool-climate greens flourish when the seasons change. The synergies that result from companion planting help to mitigate the negative effects of climate change by fostering the development of protected interdependencies.

Because of the yearly fluctuations, flexibility is of the utmost importance. When faced with unknown influences, adaptability shines through as a useful alternative to rigidity. Strengthening one's resilience through the face of unavoidable obstacles is essential to ensuring the continuation of nutrition. The cultivation of enduring, mutually beneficial partnerships that give fruit in spite of challenges requires an understanding of environmental partners.

The following are some additional considerations to keep in mind while matching plants to their environments:

- Have an understanding of the microclimates that are produced by buildings such as walls, pavement, and fences, which reflect heat and change the light and shadow patterns. Take advantage of these gaps in the market to lengthen the seasons.

- Give careful thought to the sun and shadow requirements. The majority of veggies require more than six hours of daily direct sunlight in order to grow. Tomatoes are less tolerant of being partially shaded than greens like lettuce are.

- Take into account the wind and the altitudes. In exposed places, you'll want to choose plants that can withstand the wind, while high-altitude gardens are best suited to types that are used to the lower temperatures.

- Keep an eye on the temps in each of the garden beds to determine the different microclimates. Warming and chilling are both influenced by the kind of soil, so make appropriate adjustments.

- Determine your requirements for rainfall and irrigation. Arid regions are ideally suited for the water-saving strategies of xeriscaping. In Mediterranean climes, when the winters are moist but the summers are dry, drip irrigation systems are used to supplement the rain.

- Learn the dates of your first and final frosts so you can time your plants properly. Heat-loving crops are planted after the threat of frost has passed, whereas cool-weather vegetables are planted earlier.

- Investigate the effects of the soil drainage. Raised beds, berms, and swales all change the circumstances of how wet or dry they are, which helps optimize the plant combinations.

- Pay attention to the frequent pests in your location, and select cultivars that are resistant to the specific issues that are widespread there.

A successful coupling of the plant and the climate both helps to avoid disappointment and increases the potential for yield.

- Get familiar with the USDA plant hardiness zone for your region, which is determined by the annual lowest temperatures on average. With the use of this indication, acceptable kinds may be narrowed down.

- Think about creating different microclimates around the garden. It's possible that areas enclosed by fences or structures are half a zone warmer, making it possible for more delicate plants to flourish there.

- Using a soil thermometer, you should keep an eye on the temperatures in each bed in order to determine the different microclimates. Conditions might be quite different from one location to the next.

- Be aware of the length of your growth season. Which crops have enough time to grow before the first fall frost is determined by this. Pick short-season cultivars when gardening in a marginal location.

- Analyze the patterns of the precipitation. Gardens located in arid zones require careful and effective watering. People who live in areas that have wet springs but dry summers can require additional water during the peak growing seasons for vegetables.

- Take into account the effects of height. Gardens located at higher altitudes experience shorter growing seasons and lower average nightly temperatures, which need the use of suited plant types.

- Take note of the predominant winds, and provide appropriate protection for plants that are susceptible to damage. Windbreaks prevent harm to more sensitive plants, such as herbs and greens.

Whenever the local conditions are conducive to the growth of common diseases, choose for disease-resistant kinds. Having knowledge helps one avoid feeling let down and wasting time.

- It is important to test the soil drainage in each bed, as areas with poor drainage may need raised beds or other changes to be suitable for growing crops.

Awareness of the garden's microclimate increases the potential yield by allowing the gardener to create the ideal plant alliance for the specific conditions of the garden.

Recommended crops for each season

Selecting the appropriate crops for each growing season is one of the most important aspects of successful gardening. A garden that has been carefully managed may give fresh produce that is good for you throughout the whole year. You will be able to organize your garden in an appropriate manner if you have a working knowledge of the life cycle of various crops and the seasons in which they thrive.

Crops of the Spring
The beginning of anything fresh always occurs in the spring. The weather is getting warmer, which along with the longer hours of daylight, creates excellent circumstances for many types of vegetables. The springtime is the ideal time to cultivate plants that thrive in cooler temperatures and can endure a small dusting of frost.

1. Lettuce is a leafy green that reaches maturity rapidly and does particularly well in the milder temperatures of spring. There is a wide selection available, and some of the kinds you may choose from are romaine, butterhead, and leaf lettuce.

2. Radishes: Radishes are well-known for their quick development, and it is possible to harvest them just four weeks after sowing them. They thrive in chilly climates and lend an interesting crunch and peppery flavor to spring salads.

3. The spring is an ideal time to plant legumes that have a cool-season growth cycle, such as peas. In the spring, when the soil can first be worked after the winter, they should be planted as soon as possible.

Crops for the Summer
When the weather starts to climb, it's time to start thinking about warm-season veggies. These plants can only flourish in environments with long, hot days and warm soil.

1. Tomatoes are the archetypal summer food, and in order for them to thrive, the soil in which they are grown must be warm.

2. The high temperatures of July are ideal for the growth of cucumbers. Cucumbers are versatile vegetables that may be eaten fresh, pickled, or used in salads. Cucumbers offer a satisfying crunch.

3. Both sweet and spicy peppers thrive when exposed to a high level of heat. They also require a lengthy growth season and an abundance of sunlight.

Crops for the Fall
When the oppressive heat of summer finally begins to abate, it is time to sow vegetables in preparation for a harvest in the autumn. The majority of the crops that are harvested in the spring may be replanted and cultivated for another harvest in the fall.

1. Carrots: If you plant carrots in the middle to late of summer, you can get a harvest of carrots that are tasty and crisp in the fall. Their sweetness is heightened when exposed to cooler temperatures.

2. Kale: This tenacious leafy green can be sown in the late summer for a harvest in the late fall and early winter. After being exposed to frost, the flavor really improves.

3. Beets: Beets that are planted in the late summer will develop in the fall when the weather is colder, offering a flavor that is both sweet and earthy.

The harvest of winter crops
Some plant species are hardy enough to last the winter months, particularly when grown in regions with milder winters or when given the shelter of a cold frame or greenhouse.

1. *Winter Squash*: *Winter Squash* is a type of squash that, according to its name, is harvested in the late fall and then kept so that it may be used all through the winter.

2. Brussels Sprouts: These hardy plants are able to endure cold and may be gathered throughout the winter months in a number of different places.

3. Leeks: Leeks are exceptionally resistant to frost and may be kept in the ground until they are harvested; as a result, they can be a source of fresh vegetables even throughout the winter months.

Keep in mind that these are only some suggestions. The precise plant kinds that will do well in your garden are going to be determined by the climate and weather patterns that prevail in your area. As you gain more knowledge and experience, you will discover more about what works best in the specific conditions of your garden.

Of course, it is not essential to plant crops throughout every single growing season. It is possible that giving the soil a break and then reviving it with cover crops will be helpful to the health of the garden over the long run. You should also give some thought to planting perennials in your garden, such as berry bushes, rhubarb, or asparagus, all of which will offer you with a harvest year after year with very little work on your part.

The cyclical nature of gardening is one of its most appealing aspects, since each season brings its own special rewards for those who participate. You may eat a wide variety of fruits and vegetables throughout the year if you design your garden to include crops that are grown during different seasons. As you take care of your plants from the time they are seeds until they are harvested, you will forge a closer connection not just with the food you consume but also with the cycles that occur in nature. This connection, and the delight that it produces, is the genuine treasure that the garden bestows upon its visitors.

A Better Understanding of the Climate in Your Region

The climate of your region is one of the most important factors to consider when deciding which crops will be successful. Learning your garden's USDA hardiness zone can offer you with vital information into which plants have the best chance of thriving in your particular growing conditions. The map of the USDA hardiness zone splits North America into 11 distinct zones; each zone is 10 degrees Fahrenheit warmer (or colder) in a typical winter than the zone to its immediate left or right. Once you have determined your zone, you will be able to select plants that have been assessed as suitable for the circumstances in your location.

How to Make Your Garden Look Its Best Throughout the Four Seasons

It takes careful planning to establish a garden that produces food throughout the entire year. You will want to take into consideration a variety of things, such as the quantity of sunshine that your garden gets, the quality of your soil, and the amount of water that each plant need.

Consider the following advice in order to get the most out of your garden throughout each season:
- In the spring, you should get the soil ready for planting by working in some compost or other organic waste. This will give essential nutrients for your plants. As soon as the soil can be worked, it is time to start planting your early-season crops.

- During the summer, you should make sure that your plants receive a enough amount of water, particularly during periods of dry weather. The usage of mulch can help to retain moisture and suppress the development of weeds.

- The fall season marks the beginning of harvesting late season producers and the planting of winter crops. You may also plant garlic and onions that will overwinter now in order to have a crop the following year.

- Winter: In regions with more temperate winters, it is possible to continue harvesting winter crops. If you live in a place with a shorter growing season, you might want to think about investing in a greenhouse or a cold frame.

The significance of rotating different types of crops
The rotation of crops is a fundamental agricultural activity that must be carried out in order to preserve the fertility of the soil. Changing the kinds of crops that are cultivated in a certain region on an annual basis is a component of this practice. This can help restore the soil's nutrients and avoid the growth of certain pests and illnesses that are attracted to particular plant species.

The nutritional needs, as well as the pest and disease profiles, for various crops might vary greatly. You may assist to restore nutritional balance to the soil and disrupt the life cycles of any pests or illnesses that may be present by rotating the crops that you grow.

Create a basic plan for crop rotation by dividing your garden into pieces and planting a new kind of vegetable (root, leaf, fruit, and legume) in each portion of the garden each year. This will allow you to rotate your crops more effectively. For instance, if you planted root vegetables like potatoes or carrots in one portion this year, you may switch to planting green vegetables like lettuce or spinach in that region for the next year.

Utilizing Long-Term Plants (Perennials)
Although annual crops have received the majority of attention in this discussion, the importance of perennial plants to a garden should not be discounted. Plants that live for more than two years and generate yields during each season are referred to as perennials. Perennial plants include a wide variety of herbs as well as asparagus and rhubarb. Once established, perennials require less maintenance than annuals and have the potential to produce a crop that is consistent year after year.

The activity of gardening is a dynamic and satisfying pursuit that presents new obstacles and new opportunities with the change of each season. You'll find that as you gain more experience and knowledge, the cycle of planting, growing, harvesting, and preparing the land for the next cycle becomes a satisfying and rewarding part of your life. This discovery will occur as you progress through the many stages of the cycle.

Book 2 - Using Structures to Extend the Growing Season

Cold frames, hoop houses and greenhouses

Gardening isn't just for the warmer months. With the right equipment and planning, you can grow and harvest crops year-round, even in cold climates. Cold frames, hoop houses, and greenhouses are three tools that can extend your growing season, protect your plants from harsh weather, and even allow you to grow plants that wouldn't normally thrive in your climate.

Cold Frames
Think of a cold frame as a mini greenhouse. It's essentially a box with a transparent top that allows sunlight in while protecting your plants from the elements. It keeps the soil and air inside warmer than the outside environment, which can extend your growing season by several weeks.

1. Building a Cold Frame: You can build a cold frame using a variety of materials. The frame can be made from wood, brick, or even bales of straw. The top, or lid, should be made from a transparent material like glass or clear plastic to let sunlight in. The back of the cold frame should be taller than the front to allow sunlight to reach all parts of the interior.

2. Using a Cold Frame: You can use a cold frame to start seeds earlier in the spring, keep plants growing later in the fall, or even grow cold-tolerant crops throughout the winter. Be sure to monitor the temperature inside the cold frame, as it can get too hot on sunny days. Simply lift the lid to allow excess heat to escape.

Hoop Houses
Hoop houses, also known as high tunnels, are larger than cold frames and allow you to walk inside. They are typically made from a series of hoops covered with a layer of clear plastic.

1. Building a Hoop House: To build a hoop house, you'll need flexible piping or metal rods to create the hoops, wooden boards for the base, and clear plastic sheeting to cover the structure. The ends of the hoop house are usually made from solid wood and may include doors or vents for temperature control.

2. Using a Hoop House: Hoop houses can be used to extend the growing season in spring and fall. They can also protect delicate crops from harsh weather conditions. Because of their size, they are ideal for growing large crops like tomatoes, peppers, and cucumbers.

Greenhouses
Greenhouses are the largest and most permanent of the three structures. They are designed to create an optimal growing environment that can support plants year-round.

1. Building a Greenhouse: Building a greenhouse can be a significant project. It requires a sturdy frame, typically made from metal or wood, and transparent panels made from glass or plastic. Most greenhouses also have ventilation systems to control temperature and humidity, and some include heating systems for use in the winter.

2. Using a Greenhouse: A greenhouse can be used to grow plants throughout the year. This includes starting seeds in the spring, growing heat-loving crops in the summer, extending the growing season in the fall, and growing cold-tolerant crops in the winter.

Each of these structures offers unique benefits and can be used in different ways to extend your growing season, protect your plants, and enhance your gardening experience.
However, it's important to remember that these structures are just tools. They can create more favorable conditions for your plants, but they can't replace good gardening practices. You still need to choose the right plants for your climate, prepare your soil properly, and provide your plants with the right amount and type of water and nutrients.
Gardening is as much an art as it is a science. It requires patience, observation, and a willingness to learn from both successes and failures. Whether you're using a cold frame, hoop house, or

greenhouse, remember that the most important factors in your garden's success are your care, attention, and passion.

As we explore the world of indoor gardening, it's worth noting the concept of vertical gardening. This innovative approach allows you to grow plants vertically, making the most out of your available space. This technique can be particularly beneficial in greenhouses, where space can be limited. By growing plants upward, on structures such as trellises or in hanging containers, you can increase your yield without requiring more ground space. It's an excellent strategy to keep in mind as you plan and optimize your indoor gardening structures.

Heating and ventilation systems

The use of unheated buildings for harvesting purposes throughout the year is made possible by reliable temperature management. In this article, I discuss the findings of my experiments with a variety of systems that have been customized to livable growth spaces: I was able to build a commercial-grade furnace when my budget allowed for it, which enabled me to increase my output. Dual thermostats allow the living quarters and the growing areas to be independently controlled according to the requirements of the plants and the people. During periods of extreme cold, extensive venting removes moisture from the system while piping heats the roots. Infrared heat lamps may be purchased at a lower cost and emit heat in a particular direction onto crops. Fixtures that hang from the ceiling remove leaves without drying out the air. Timers ensure that temperatures are kept at the optimum level to prevent energy waste during the daytime when sunshine is sufficient. Insulation that reflects light enhances its impact.

When it comes to performance, bottom heat is superior to variants that are hung overhead for smaller gardens. Because heat rises, however, roots capes can be effectively supported by warm flooring despite the presence of ice. When compared to more expensive whole-structure systems, thermostatic mats are a cost-effective method for reviving seedlings.

The use of pillars of passive solar architecture reduces the need for power. Large windows that face south are best for capturing heat, which may then be stored in masonry or water mass for slow evening radiation. Vents quickly remove extra warm air while maintaining the appropriate temperature inside.

Diseases are less likely to develop in an environment with adequate ventilation than one that is moist and stagnant. Fresh air is brought in through intake vents, and exhaust air is drawn out by extractor fans in response to readings from adjustable hygrometers. When vents are placed in opposite directions, cross breezes are created.

Every strategy is tailored to a unique set of objectives and finances. The necessity of efficiency in maintaining sustainability was learned via trial and error; the ductwork that moves heat turns out to be more significant than its source. With refinement comes empowerment over, which unlocks the intrinsic ability of vegetables to be consumed throughout the year.

Installing shade structures

The right amount of sun exposure is vital for the growth and well-being of plants. While many plants revel in the sunlight, some prefer to stay in the shade. In places where the sun is too harsh, or where delicate plants need to be grown, installing a shade structure becomes essential. This chapter will guide you through selecting, designing, and installing shade structures in your garden to protect your plants and enhance your garden's aesthetic appeal.

Understanding the Role of Shade Structures
Shade structures, as their name suggests, are structures designed to provide shade. They can shield your plants from intense sunlight, reduce water evaporation, and create a cooler, more humid environment that some plants prefer. Shade structures come in various forms, from simple shade cloth structures to more sophisticated pergolas and gazebos.

Assessing Your Garden's Needs
Before you start designing and installing shade structures, it's important to understand your garden's needs. Here's a simple process to follow:

1. Identify Sun-Sensitive Plants: Research the plants you have or plan to add to your garden. Identify which ones prefer shade or partial shade and group them together.

2. Monitor Sun Exposure: Spend a few days observing your garden at different times. Note the areas that receive the most sun and the areas that are naturally shaded.

3. Decide on the Type of Structure: Depending on the level of shade needed, the area to be covered, and your garden's style, decide on the type of shade structure that would be best.

Types of Shade Structures
There are several types of shade structures you can consider:

1. Shade Cloth Structures: These are simple structures made by draping a shade cloth over a frame. They are easy to install and can be moved around as needed.

2. Pergolas: Pergolas are larger, more permanent structures. They can provide partial to full shade, depending on the spacing of the overhead beams and whether they are covered with a shade cloth or climbing plants.

3. Gazebos: Gazebos are freestanding structures that provide full shade. They can be a beautiful addition to a garden, but they are also more costly and time-consuming to install.

4. Tree Shade: Planting trees can be a natural way to provide shade. However, keep in mind that trees take several years to grow large enough to offer substantial shade.

Installing Shade Structures
The process of installing your shade structure will depend on the type you have chosen.

1. Location: Choose a location that provides the right amount of shade for the plants you are protecting. This might mean installing

the shade structure over existing plants or moving plants to the shaded location.

2. Size and Orientation: The size of your shade structure will depend on the number of plants you need to protect and the space available in your garden. The orientation should be such that it provides maximum shade when the sun is at its peak.

3. Material: Choose a material that provides the right amount of shade and is durable enough to withstand your local weather conditions. For example, a shade cloth with a higher percentage will block more sunlight.

4. Installation: For simple shade cloth structures, installation might be as easy as erecting some posts and draping the shade cloth over them. For more complex structures like pergolas and gazebos, you might need to hire a professional or follow detailed DIY instructions.

Shade structures can do more than just provide shade. They can also be a focal point in your garden, adding to its aesthetic appeal. Consider adding features like seating areas under gazebos or training climbing plants up pergolas to create a beautiful and functional garden oasis.

As you plan your garden's layout, it's essential to consider the growth patterns and sunlight needs of different plants. The right placement can help your plants thrive while creating a visually appealing landscape. For instance, placing taller plants on the north side of your garden can provide natural shade for sun-sensitive plants. Similarly, plants that require full sun should not be placed under a shade structure unless it's designed to allow a certain amount of sunlight to pass through. Good planning and careful consideration can help create a balanced ecosystem in your garden, promoting healthier, happier plants.

Frost protection strategies

Dedicated gardening requires taking precautions to protect crops that are susceptible to damage when temperatures drop. The following are some strategies that have been established via a variety of experiences:

A row cover made of cloth that is stretched loosely over hoops can maintain the necessary temperature while yet allowing airflow. Spun bond fabric that is thinner can tolerate freezing while still allowing sunlight through for photosynthesis, whereas Ree may fabric that is thicker can retain more heat at the expense of light transmission. Either one will do for little periods of perseverance.

Sheltering seedlings during the establishing phase with hot caps made from plastic gallon jugs with the bottoms cut out focuses sunlight, which in turn warms the plants naturally. The function of the tiny hothouses is comparable to that of a miniature version of either a high or low tunnel.

Floating row cover cloth on top of plants minimizes direct contact, allowing removal in the event that unexpectedly high heat spikes develop. This reduces the regular risk of freezing under the row cover, as was unfortunately learned in 2016.

Alongside the beds, the process of trenching creates small furrows into which coarse cloth drapes and accumulates. It is anchored at ground level, and throughout the night it emits the warmth that has been building. Drainage protects against the most catastrophic of outcomes by avoiding the occurrence of flooded roots.

Woody litter or moveable mulches can be used to cover temperature-sensitive crops and protect them from the kiss of frost. Light barriers prevent radiative freezing and keep crucial temperatures well above the limits at which it becomes fatal. Through trial and error, one may determine the best times to apply and remove a substance.

Heat may be retained in hollow buildings such as hoop tunnels and Quonset huts without the need for resources such as thermostatic drainage systems. For the sake of sitting, planning is required.

Book 3 - Building Fertile Soil for Optimal Plant Health

The importance of organic matter and compost

Gardening is much more than just planting seeds and waiting for them to grow. It involves creating an environment where plants can thrive, and a key part of that environment is the soil. Organic matter and compost play a crucial role in enriching the soil and providing the nutrients plants need to grow. They improve the soil structure, feed soil microbes, and help retain moisture.

The Role of Organic Matter in Soil
Organic matter is any material that was once alive and is now in or on the soil. It can come from plants, animals, or microorganisms. Here are three ways organic matter contributes to a healthy soil:

1. Nutrient Supply: Organic matter is rich in essential nutrients that plants need, such as nitrogen, phosphorus, and potassium. As the organic matter breaks down, these nutrients are released into the soil.

2. Water Retention: Organic matter can absorb and hold water, making it available to plants. This is especially important in sandy soils, which tend to drain quickly.

3. Soil Structure Improvement: Organic matter helps bind soil particles together, creating a crumbly structure that is easy for plant roots to penetrate. It also prevents soil from compacting and improves its ability to resist erosion.

The Role of Compost in Soil
Compost is decomposed organic matter. It is created through a process called composting, where organic waste materials like leaves, grass clippings, and kitchen scraps are broken down by microorganisms. Here are three reasons why compost is beneficial:

1. Rich in Nutrients: Compost is often called "black gold" because of its rich nutrient content. It contains a variety of nutrients that plants need, and these nutrients are released slowly over time, providing a steady supply to plants.

2. Improves Soil Structure: Like organic matter, compost can improve the structure of the soil, making it easier for plant roots to grow. It can also help sandy soils hold more water and help clay soils drain better.

3. Boosts Soil Microbes: Compost is teeming with beneficial microorganisms that can help suppress plant diseases. These microbes also continue the process of breaking down organic matter in the soil, releasing even more nutrients for plants.

Making and Using Compost
Making your own compost is a practical and cost-effective way to provide your garden with rich, organic material. It's also an excellent way to recycle kitchen and garden waste. Here's a basic guide on how to make and use compost:

1. Building a Compost Pile: Choose a suitable location in your yard and start your compost pile directly on the ground. Start with a layer of coarse brown material (like twigs) to aid drainage, then alternate between layers of green material (like vegetable scraps) and brown material (like dried leaves).

2. Maintaining the Compost Pile: Turn your compost pile every few weeks using a pitchfork or shovel. This helps aerate the pile and speeds up the composting process. The compost is ready when it looks, feels, and smells like rich, dark earth.

3. Using Compost in Your Garden: Add a layer of compost to your garden beds each season before planting. You can also use compost as a mulch around established plants.

While organic matter and compost are vital for soil health, it's essential to remember that different plants have different nutrient needs. Some plants might thrive in a soil enriched with compost while others might prefer a leaner soil. Always research the specific needs of the plants in your garden and adjust your soil improvement practices accordingly.

In addition to improving the soil and providing nutrients, organic matter and compost can also play a significant role in sustainable gardening practices. They help reduce the amount of organic waste that ends up in landfills and decrease the need for chemical fertilizers, which can have negative environmental impacts. By making and using compost, you're not only nurturing your garden but also contributing to a healthier, more sustainable planet.

Testing and amending soil pH and nutrients

Greenery thrives when the soil's equilibrium is restored. At first, the parameters were puzzling despite the fact that fertility appeared to be abundant; the fact that the crops were weak prompted us to examine the complicated dance of the rootzones. I will provide the following methods for locating imbalances:

Naturally acidic soils are a problem in my location, which reduces the amount of nutrients that are available and their solubility. An cheap pH meter turned out to be a worthwhile purchase by discovering harmful 5.0 levels. Lime was used to progressively sweeten the landscape in a sustainable manner according to the guidelines. Micronutrient deficits manifested itself as telltale signs, such as lime lockouts, which leached boron, and magnesium chlorosis, which reacted swiftly to foliar applications of Epsom salts. Following that, testing carried out by extension services revealed certain deficiencies that might be easily and reasonably addressed.

The nitrogen, phosphorus, and potassium levels in the soil are evaluated annually using Ronseal kit testing. Color comparisons provide an approximation of quantities, allowing one to prevent under- or over-fertilizing in accordance with their requirements. Applications of compost, which provide homogeneous nutrients, blur the lines between different areas.

Exploring the cation exchange capability and revealing the hidden complexities informed the changes. Sandier soils require organic matter that can hold onto a greater quantity of minerals, whereas clays must have an abundance of magnesium, calcium, and potassium. Having an understanding of the gardening needs of each location.

Taking part in university soil samples allowed for a second pair of eyes to examine the soil's precise make-up. Inadequate zinc or an excess of sodium as a result of road salt were identified as causes of drainage problems in the recommendations. The customization of correctives minimized the expenditures.

The natural state of equilibrium may be maintained with consistent monitoring. When errors are corrected gradually, they do not startle the microorganisms. As decomposers transform dead matter into nutrients essential to life, a thriving community eventually becomes self-sufficient. The preservation of soil assets via stewardship promotes the health of plant life.

Fertilization needs by season

Gardening is an art of timing and balance, especially when it comes to fertilization. Providing your plants with the nutrients they need at the right time can significantly enhance their growth and productivity. However, the needs of your garden can change from season to season, and understanding these changes is key to effective fertilization.

Understanding Fertilizer Basics
Before diving into seasonal fertilization strategies, it's important to understand the basics of fertilizers. Most complete fertilizers contain three primary nutrients that plants need in large quantities:
- Nitrogen (N): Promotes leafy green growth.
- Phosphorus (P): Supports root development, flowering, and fruiting.
- Potassium (K): Enhances overall plant health and resistance to diseases and pests.
Fertilizers can be organic (derived from plant or animal sources) or synthetic (manufactured chemically). Both types have their pros and cons, and the choice between them often comes down to personal preference and specific garden needs.

Spring Fertilization
Spring is a time of rapid growth for many plants, and they often need an extra boost of nutrients to support this growth:

- Nitrogen: Since spring is a time of leafy growth, a higher amount of nitrogen can be beneficial. Consider using a balanced fertilizer with a higher first number (N).
- Phosphorus and Potassium: These nutrients are also important in spring to support root growth and plant health as plants come out of their winter dormancy.

Summer Fertilization
In the summer, the focus often shifts from growth to maintenance:
- Nitrogen: Too much nitrogen in the summer can lead to excessive leafy growth at the expense of flowers and fruits. Consider reducing nitrogen application during this period, especially for fruiting and flowering plants.
- Phosphorus and Potassium: Continue to provide these nutrients to support ongoing root development, flowering, and fruiting.

Fall Fertilization
Fall is a time to prepare your garden for the coming winter:
- Nitrogen: Reduce nitrogen application in the fall to avoid promoting new growth that could be damaged by winter cold.
- Phosphorus and Potassium: These nutrients can help strengthen plants and prepare them for winter. Consider a fertilizer with a higher last number (K) in the fall.

Winter Fertilization
In most climates, plants go dormant in the winter, and their nutrient needs are minimal:
- All Nutrients: It's usually best to limit fertilization in the winter to avoid stimulating growth that the winter cold could damage.

Tailoring Fertilization to Your Garden
While the above guidelines can provide a general roadmap, the specific fertilization needs of your garden can vary based on many factors, including the types of plants you're growing, your local climate, and your soil type. Always observe your plants and adjust your fertilization practices as needed based on their response.
Keep in mind that over-fertilization can be just as harmful as under-fertilization. Too much fertilizer can lead to excessive, weak growth, burn plant roots, and even contribute to water pollution. Always follow

package instructions when applying fertilizer, and consider getting a soil test to understand your soil's specific nutrient needs.

Your fertilization strategy should also consider the environmental impact. Using organic fertilizers or making your own compost can help reduce the environmental footprint of your garden. These practices not only provide nutrients but also improve soil structure, promote soil life, and recycle waste.

While a lot of attention is given to the role of fertilizers, it's worth remembering that they are only one part of a plant's growth equation. Other factors such as light, water, temperature, and overall care are equally, if not more, important. In fact, a healthy plant grown in well-tended soil may require very little additional fertilizer. Therefore, always consider fertilization as part of a broader, holistic approach to gardening.

Cover crops and green manures

In the world of gardening and farming, there's a secret weapon that can help to improve soil fertility and suppress weeds, all while reducing the need for chemical fertilizers and herbicides. This powerful tool is the use of cover crops and green manures. These plant allies are cultivated specifically to benefit the soil and provide a myriad of advantages for both small-scale and large-scale cultivation.

Understanding Cover Crops and Green Manures
Cover crops and green manures are types of crops that are grown primarily for the benefit of the soil rather than for harvest. While the terms are often used interchangeably, there is a subtle difference between them:

- Cover Crops: These are crops grown to cover the soil and protect it from erosion and weed growth. They can be left to grow over winter, turned under in the spring, or used as a living mulch during the growing season.

- Green Manures: These are crops that are grown and then turned under while they're still green. The purpose of green manures is to add organic matter and nutrients to the soil.

Benefits of Growing Cover Crops and Green Manures

Growing cover crops and green manures can bring numerous benefits to your garden:

1. Soil Fertility: They add organic matter and nutrients to the soil, improving its fertility.

2. Weed Control: By covering the soil, they prevent weeds from getting the light and space they need to grow.

3. Erosion Prevention: They protect the soil from being washed or blown away by the elements.

4. Pest Management: Certain cover crops can deter pests or attract beneficial insects.

Choosing and Growing Cover Crops and Green Manures
The choice of cover crop or green manure depends on your specific needs, the time of year, and your local climate. Here are some popular choices:
- Legumes: Crops like clover, vetch, and peas add nitrogen to the soil, a nutrient that many plants need in large quantities.
- Grasses: Crops like rye, oats, and barley are excellent at adding organic matter to the soil and suppressing weed growth.
- Brassicas: Crops like mustard and rapeseed can help control soil-borne pests and diseases.
To grow cover crops and green manures, you simply sow the seeds in the area where you want to improve the soil. If you're using the crops as green manure, you'll need to turn them under before they go to seed. This is usually done a few weeks before you plan to plant your main crops.

Incorporating Cover Crops and Green Manures into Your Gardening Practices
Cover crops and green manures can be a valuable addition to any garden or farm. Here are a few ways to incorporate them into your gardening practices:

1. Off-Season Planting: Plant cover crops in the fall after harvesting your main crops. This will protect your soil over the winter and provide you with a green manure to turn under in the spring.

2. Interplanting: Plant cover crops in between rows of your main crops. This can help suppress weeds and can also provide living mulch that helps retain soil moisture.

3. Rotation: Use cover crops and green manures as part of a crop rotation schedule. This can help break up disease and pest cycles and improve soil fertility.

While cover crops and green manures can greatly enhance soil health and productivity, it's essential to remember that they are just one part of a broader soil management strategy. Other practices such as composting, mulching, and proper irrigation are also important for maintaining healthy soil.

Besides their soil-improving qualities, cover crops and green manures also contribute to biodiversity by providing habitats and food sources for a variety of wildlife. From pollinators attracted to the flowering cover crops to birds feasting on the seeds, these plants play a crucial role in supporting a vibrant and diverse ecosystem. Therefore, they're not only a smart choice for the health of your garden but also a great way to support local wildlife and contribute to a healthier planet.

Book 4 - Watering Methods for Efficient Irrigation

Drip irrigation, soaker hoses, and sprinklers

Greenery thrives when the soil's equilibrium is restored. At first, the parameters were puzzling despite the fact that fertility appeared to be abundant; the fact that the crops were weak prompted us to examine the complicated dance of the rootzones. I will provide the following methods for locating imbalances:

Naturally acidic soils are a problem in my location, which reduces the amount of nutrients that are available and their solubility. An cheap pH meter turned out to be a worthwhile purchase by discovering harmful 5.0 levels. Lime was used to progressively sweeten the landscape in a sustainable manner according to the guidelines. Micronutrient deficits manifested itself as telltale signs, such as lime lockouts, which leached boron, and magnesium chlorosis, which reacted swiftly to foliar applications of Epsom salts. Following that, testing carried out by extension services revealed certain deficiencies that might be easily and reasonably addressed.

However, the delivery of water from above results in significant volume loss. Water is the elixir of life for plants. The use of porous tubing that is clipped across rows and then buried an inch below allows for drip irrigation to evenly wet rhizospheres. The emitters spray the areas that need it, preventing either overwatering or underwatering.

If you attach soaker hoses to the soil contours, they will wrap the roots for several hours and absorb the runoff that mulches would otherwise cause. Timers keep a consistent rhythm going without making the work boring. Switching from spray nozzles that are harsh on the vegetation and compress the topsoil is encouraged by the savings.

The softness of rain simulation, as opposed to bombardment, is what makes an occasional soaking effective in reviving wilting. Aerating planting material and oxygenating micro herds while simultaneously replenishing canopies from below is what nature had in mind when she designed the system. The practice of conservation evolves into the cornerstone of agricultural philosophy.

Setting up rainwater collection systems

Harnessing the power of nature to meet our needs is a practice as old as humanity itself. In the quest for self-sustainability, one of the most accessible and beneficial steps you can take is setting up a rainwater collection system. This can help you conserve water, save money, and make the most of a natural resource.

Understanding Rainwater Collection
Rainwater collection, also known as rainwater harvesting, is the practice of collecting and storing rainwater for later use. This can be as simple as positioning a barrel under a downspout, or as complex as a system with tanks, pumps, and filtration.
Rainwater can be used for a variety of purposes, such as watering gardens, washing cars, or even for drinking, provided it's properly treated. It's a free source of soft, chlorine-free water that can reduce your reliance on municipal water supplies.

Benefits of Rainwater Collection
Collecting rainwater comes with several benefits:

1. Water Conservation: Rainwater collection can reduce your use of municipal water, conserving a precious resource.
2. Financial Savings: By reducing your water usage, you can save on your water bills.
3. Plant Health: Rainwater is free from the chlorine and other chemicals found in tap water, which can be beneficial for plants.
4. Flood Prevention: Collecting rainwater can help reduce runoff, which can help prevent flooding and erosion.

Components of a Rainwater Collection System
A basic rainwater collection system typically includes the following components:
1. Catchment Area: This is usually the roof of your house or another structure. The water is channeled into the collection system through gutters and downspouts.

2. First-Flush Diverter: This device diverts the first flow of rainwater, which may contain debris or bird droppings from the roof, away from the storage tank.

3. Storage Tank or Barrel: This is where the rainwater is stored. Tanks can be above or below ground and can range in size from a small barrel to a large cistern.

4. Delivery System: This can be as simple as a spigot on the bottom of a barrel, or as complex as a pump and irrigation system.

5. Treatment System: If the water is to be used for drinking, it will need to be treated to remove any potential pathogens.

Setting Up a Basic Rainwater Collection System
Here's a simple step-by-step guide to setting up a basic rainwater barrel system:

1. Choose Your Barrel: Look for a barrel that's made from food-grade or otherwise non-toxic materials. The barrel should have a spigot near the bottom and a screen on top to keep out debris and mosquitoes.

2. Position Your Barrel: Place the barrel under a downspout. You may want to place it on a stand for easier access to the spigot.

3. Install a Diverter: Install a downspout diverter to direct water into the barrel. The diverter should automatically bypass the barrel when it's full.

4. Connect a Hose: Connect a hose to the spigot for watering, or simply fill up watering cans.

5. Cover and Maintain: Make sure the top of the barrel is covered to prevent mosquitoes and debris. Check and clean your system regularly to ensure it's working properly.

Legal Considerations
Before setting up a rainwater collection system, it's important to check local regulations. Some areas have restrictions on rainwater

collection, often related to water rights laws. It's essential to ensure your system is legal and meets any required guidelines or standards.

Expanding Your System
Once you've set up a basic system, there are many ways you could expand or upgrade it. For instance, you could add more barrels to increase your storage capacity. You could install a pump to deliver water to parts of your property that aren't gravity-fed. If you're interested in using rainwater inside your home or for drinking, you could explore options for filtration and disinfection.
In addition to its practical benefits, setting up a rainwater collection system can be a rewarding project that helps you connect with the natural water cycle. It's an opportunity to take practical action towards sustainability. And each time you water your plants with collected rainwater, or see your barrels filling up during a storm, you'll have the satisfaction of knowing you're making the most of nature's gifts.

Techniques for reducing water usage

Because of the unpredictability of the climate, conservation is now an absolute need. In this context, methods of sustainability emerged through experience:
The use of mulch creates a covering over the soil, which lowers temperatures and reduces evaporation. However, plastic or landscape fabric only have a short-term purpose, whereas organic materials feed the soil as they age. Under vegetable patches, a depth of two inches is sufficient.
Capillary action brings about a gradual process of hydration in composted amendments. When compared to moisture-holding organics, which energize soil lifecycles, granular fertilizers drain quickly, which results in the need for excessive watering.
Irrigation with a drip system can identify exactly where water is required. In contrast to sprinklers, which are inefficiently spraying the vegetation, porous tubing absorbs effusively beside the rows. The emitters are designed to target the roots that are burrowing deeper as opposed to the surface-wetted topsoil.
The collection of rainwater from roof gutters helps to replenish reserves for times of drought. Cisterns are used to supplement the

municipal supplies that are intermittently available. Self-sufficiency has been replaced by reliance. Swales direct excess water away from flooded carpets, preventing the carpets from losing moisture underneath.

The alignment of contours achieved by terracing beds prevents runoff from being strong enough to erode vital topsoil. Ridges that are confined inside their own boundaries optimize the effects of each droplet, hence conserving fertility.

Microclimates, such as those created by mulched paths, are left untouched, allowing rainwater to seep into the planting beds below and organically redistribute itself rather than being diverted away as runoff. The intentionality of anything mimics the efficacy of nature.

Mulching to retain moisture

In the world of gardening, mulching is a practice that is both simple and powerful. By laying down a layer of organic or inorganic material around your plants, you can conserve soil moisture, regulate soil temperature, suppress weeds, and enrich the soil. This chapter will provide you with practical advice on using mulch to retain moisture and promote a vibrant, healthy garden.

Understanding Mulch and Its Benefits
Mulch is any material that is spread around plants or over the ground to protect or improve the soil. There are many types of mulch, ranging from organic materials like wood chips, straw, or compost, to inorganic materials like rocks, gravel, or plastic.

Mulching has several benefits:
1. Moisture Retention: Mulch slows the evaporation of water from the soil, helping to keep it moist for longer.
2. Temperature Control: By insulating the soil, mulch can help keep it cool in the summer and warm in the winter.
3. Weed Suppression: A thick layer of mulch can prevent weed seeds from germinating.
4. Soil Enrichment: Organic mulches decompose over time, adding nutrients to the soil.
5. Erosion Prevention: Mulch can protect the soil from being washed away by heavy rains.

Choosing the Right Mulch for Moisture Retention
Different types of mulch have different properties and are suited to different uses. When it comes to retaining moisture, organic mulches are generally more effective than inorganic ones. This is because they can absorb and hold moisture, whereas inorganic mulches primarily slow evaporation by shielding the soil from the sun.

Some good choices for moisture-retaining mulch include:
- Wood Chips or Bark: These are long-lasting and visually appealing. They are best for perennial beds, trees, and shrubs.
- Straw or Hay: These are lightweight and easy to spread. They are often used in vegetable gardens.
- Compost: This can enrich the soil as it mulches, but it may contain weed seeds.
- Grass Clippings: These decompose quickly and add nitrogen to the soil, but they should be used in thin layers to avoid matting.
- Leaves: These are plentiful and free in the fall. They work well when shredded and can be used in any garden area.

How to Mulch Your Garden
Applying mulch is a straightforward process, but there are a few tips and tricks that can help you get the most out of it.

1. Prepare the Soil: Before you apply mulch, remove any weeds and ensure the soil is moist.

2. Choose Your Mulch: Decide on the best type of mulch for your needs. Consider the plants, the climate, and your aesthetic preferences.

3. Apply the Mulch: Spread a layer of mulch around your plants and over the soil. The layer should be thick enough to block sunlight and prevent weeds, usually 2-4 inches.

4. Avoid the Stem: When mulching around plants, leave a small space around the stem or trunk. This prevents moisture from rotting the base of the plant.

5. Maintain the Mulch: Over time, organic mulches will decompose and will need to be replenished. Check your mulch regularly and add more as needed.

Common Mulching Mistakes to Avoid
While mulching is beneficial, it's important to avoid some common mistakes:
- Over-Mulching: Too much mulch can suffocate plants and cause root rot. Stick to a layer of 2-4 inches.
- Under-Mulching: A layer that's too thin won't suppress weeds or retain moisture effectively. Make sure your mulch covers the soil completely.
- Wrong Placement: Mulch piled against the stem or trunk of a plant can cause rot. Always leave a small, mulch-free zone around the base of each plant.
- Using Diseased Material: Mulch made from diseased plants or weeds can spread problems to your garden. Always use clean, disease-free materials for mulch.

Mulching is more than just a way to maintain soil moisture; it's a tool that can significantly enhance the health and beauty of your garden. By choosing the right mulch and applying it correctly, you can create a thriving, low-maintenance garden that saves water and resists weeds.
In addition to its immediate benefits, mulching also contributes to the long-term health and fertility of your soil. As organic mulches decompose, they become a form of compost, enriching the soil with organic matter and nutrients. This process also encourages the activity of beneficial soil organisms like earthworms and bacteria, who further enhance soil structure and fertility. Thus, the simple act of laying down mulch can set off a chain of soil-improving processes that benefit your garden for years to come. Therefore, when you mulch, you're not only nurturing your plants in the present but also investing in the future health and productivity of your garden.

Adding Diversity to Your Mulch
In nature, soil is rarely covered with just one type of material. Therefore, to mimic nature and increase the health of your garden, you might consider using a mix of different types of organic mulches.

This can provide a wider range of nutrients as the mulches break down, and can also create a more varied habitat for beneficial soil organisms. For instance, a layer of straw might be topped with a layer of compost, creating a diverse "mulch sandwich" that offers multiple benefits.

The Role of Mulch in a Water-Wise Garden
In areas where water is scarce, mulching is an essential part of creating a water-wise garden. By retaining moisture in the soil, mulch can reduce the need for watering and help plants survive during dry periods. Combining mulching with other water-saving practices, like choosing drought-tolerant plants and watering deeply but infrequently, can create a garden that's both beautiful and resilient in the face of water scarcity.

Mulching in Different Seasons
The type of mulch you use and when you apply it can change with the seasons. In the spring, a layer of compost could provide a boost of nutrients for plant growth. In the summer, straw or wood chips could help keep the soil cool and moist. In the fall, fallen leaves can be recycled into mulch that insulates the soil over winter and breaks down to enrich the soil in the spring.

Other Creative Uses for Mulch
Beyond the garden, there are other places where mulch can be beneficial. Mulch can be used to create paths through your garden, suppressing weeds and creating a soft, appealing walkway. In a chicken run, mulch can keep down dust and provide chickens with a place to scratch and forage. Around trees, a ring of mulch can protect the tree from mower damage and reduce competition from grass.

Investing in a Mulcher or Chipper
For those with large gardens or yards, it might be worth investing in a mulcher or chipper. These machines can turn tree branches, pruning, and other garden waste into wood chip mulch. This can save money on buying mulch and can also help you recycle garden waste on-site.

Mulching: A Key Part of Organic Gardening

For those interested in organic gardening, mulching is a key practice. By using organic mulches, you can build a healthy soil ecosystem that supports robust plant growth without the need for synthetic fertilizers or pesticides.

Mulching isn't just an isolated task. It's part of a holistic approach to gardening that takes into account the health of the soil, the needs of the plants, and the resources available. By understanding and harnessing the power of mulch, you can create a garden that is not only lush and productive, but also sustainable and in harmony with nature.

While we've covered a lot about mulch and its role in moisture retention, it's worth noting that mulch has aesthetic benefits too. With a variety of colors, textures, and materials available, mulch can play a key role in defining your garden's look and feel. From the rustic appeal of straw and wood chips to the polished elegance of decorative stone, mulch can be as much a part of your garden's design as the plants themselves. So while you're planning your mulching strategy, don't forget to consider the visual impact as well. After all, a garden should be a feast for the eyes just as much as it is a banquet for the plants.

Book 5 - Pest Prevention and Organic Solutions

Identifying common garden pests

Without constant monitoring, even the most robust gardens may be destroyed by pests. Despite the fact that vigorous crops are beneficial to health, they often attract opportunists when there are weaknesses. Close observation makes it easier to come up with non-chemical solutions that prevent collateral damage. The following are examples of frequent visitors:

Aphids may invade fragile new growth through a process called parthenogenesis and then drain its vitality by transmitting viruses. The natural population control provided by ladybugs is superior than that provided by pesticides, which kill beneficial insects.

Slugs are nighttime pests that cause damage to vegetation by eating it. Copper barriers or dry mulch surrounding plants discourage movement, and catching them in beer bowls protects the plants from injury.

Both cabbage worms and loopers leave behind holes as a proof of their existence through chewing. Eliminating larvae without the use of manmade toxins can be accomplished by removing affected leaves or spraying Bt.

Brassicas and nightshades are susceptible to damage by beetles. Rotation has the effect of destroying habitat, whereas handpicking is effective in getting rid of invasive Colorado potato beetles.

It is necessary to examine the plants for scars or damaged stems since cutworms and squash bugs lurk at the soil level. Protective coverings like as cloches or collars are placed around fragile transplants.

Intervention can be reduced by increased sanitary conditions and increased tolerance. The natural world is able to sustain modest loss without falling apart, and humans play an important role in maintaining ecological balance and promoting biodiversity. Being vigilant allows one to differentiate between potential dangers and natural occurrences.

Organic and natural control options

Embracing the organic approach to pest control means swapping out synthetic, chemical-based pesticides for natural methods. This shift can benefit your garden, your health, and the environment. This chapter will guide you through organic and natural control options that are both effective and environmentally friendly.

Understanding Organic Pest Control
Organic pest control involves using methods and materials which are natural, biodegradable, and don't harm the environment. These may include biological controls like predators or parasites, cultural controls like crop rotation, physical controls like barriers, and natural chemical controls like botanical pesticides.

Organic pest controls have several benefits:
- Eco-friendly: They don't contribute to chemical pollution, are safe for beneficial insects, and are usually less harmful to non-target organisms.
- Cost-effective: Many organic pest controls can be made at home or are cheaper than synthetic pesticides.
- Healthier Plants and Soil: Organic methods often improve soil health and plant vigor, making your garden more resilient to pests in the long run.

Biological Control Options
One of the most effective ways to control pests organically is to use the pests' natural enemies. These can be other insects, birds, or microorganisms.
- Beneficial Insects: Ladybugs, lacewings, and predatory mites are among the many beneficial insects that can control pests. You can attract them to your garden with the right plants, or purchase them from suppliers.
- Birds: Many birds feed on insects. Birdhouses, birdbaths, and bird feeders can attract these natural predators to your garden.
- Microorganisms: Certain bacteria, fungi, and nematodes can kill pests. Products containing these beneficial microorganisms can be sprayed on your plants.

Cultural Control Methods
Cultural controls involve changes in your gardening practices to make the environment less inviting to pests.
- Crop Rotation: Changing where you plant specific crops each year can interrupt pest life cycles.
- Diverse Plantings: A diverse garden can support beneficial insects and make it harder for pests to spread.
- Healthy Soil: Healthy plants are more resistant to pests. Composting, mulching, and proper watering can all contribute to soil health.

Physical and Mechanical Controls
Physical and mechanical controls create barriers or traps, or physically remove pests from the garden.
- Barriers: Netting, row covers, or collars can protect plants from pests.
- Traps: Traps with pheromones or visual lures can attract and capture pests.
- Handpicking: For larger pests like snails and beetles, sometimes the best solution is the simplest one: picking them off by hand.

Natural Chemical Controls
When other methods are not enough, natural chemicals derived from plants, minerals, or other natural sources can be used.
- Botanical Pesticides: These are derived from plants. For example, neem oil disrupts the life cycle of many insects.
- Mineral-based Pesticides: These include diatomaceous earth, which can kill insects by dehydrating them, and sulfur, a traditional fungicide.
- Homemade Sprays: Kitchen ingredients like garlic, chili pepper, or vinegar can deter pests.

Integrating Organic Pest Control Methods
Organic pest control is most effective when these methods are integrated. This means using a combination of biological, cultural, physical, and natural chemical controls, and adjusting your strategy based on the pests present and the time of year. This integrated approach can keep pest populations at manageable levels and prevent the need for drastic measures.

Monitoring and Identifying Pests
Before you can control pests, you need to know what you're dealing with. Regularly inspect your plants for signs of pests, and learn to identify common garden pests in your area. Remember, not all insects are harmful; some may be beneficial insects that are helping to control pests.

Understanding and Accepting Some Damage
An important part of organic pest control is accepting that some level of pest damage is normal and tolerable. It's usually not necessary or desirable to eliminate all pests from your garden. A few chewed leaves won't harm your plants, and may even attract beneficial insects.

Safety Considerations
While organic pest control methods are generally safer than synthetic pesticides, they should still be used with care. Even natural substances can be harmful if misused. Always follow the label instructions on any product, wear protective clothing when needed, and keep all pest control products out of reach of children and pets. A healthy and vibrant garden is possible without resorting to synthetic pesticides. By understanding and working with nature, rather than against it, you can keep pests in check while maintaining a garden that's healthy for you, your plants, and the environment.
Just as pests have natural enemies, they also have natural allies. Some insects, like aphids, excrete a sweet substance called honeydew that attracts ants. The ants protect the aphids from predators in order to keep the honeydew flowing. If you see ants on your plants, this may indicate an aphid problem. In this case, controlling the ants or disrupting their relationship with the aphids can help control the aphid population. This highlights the importance of understanding the relationships between different organisms in your garden. By paying attention to these interactions, you can often deal with pests in a way that is both more effective and more in tune with nature.
So, as you venture into your gardening journey, remember that organic pest control is about more than just swapping out synthetic pesticides for natural ones. It's about creating a balanced garden ecosystem that can resist pests naturally. It's about understanding the pests you're dealing with and using a combination of strategies to

manage them. And it's about accepting that a certain level of pests and pest damage is part of a healthy garden. With patience, observation, and a willingness to learn, you can successfully control pests in a way that benefits your garden, your health, and the environment.

Companion planting strategies

A garden is a vibrant and complex ecosystem, where plants interact with each other as well as the soil, insects, and other organisms. A wise gardener can harness these interactions to create a healthier, more productive garden. This is the essence of companion planting, a time-honored practice that pairs different plants together for mutual benefit.

Understanding Companion Planting
Companion planting involves growing different types of plants together so that they help each other grow. They can benefit each other in various ways, such as improving soil fertility, deterring pests, attracting beneficial insects, enhancing flavor, and saving space.

The benefits of companion planting are numerous:
- Enhanced Productivity: When plants share space, they can utilize the resources more efficiently. For instance, a tall plant can provide shade for a shorter one that prefers cooler temperatures.
- Pest Control: Some plants repel certain insects or diseases. Planting them next to vulnerable crops can protect those crops from pests.
- Improved Soil Health: Some plants, especially legumes, can enrich the soil by fixing nitrogen from the air.

Key Companion Planting Strategies
Applying companion planting strategies requires an understanding of the needs, characteristics, and potential partners of each plant. Here are some strategies that can guide your planting decisions:

- The Three Sisters: This is a traditional Native American companion planting technique that pairs corn, beans, and squash. The corn provides a structure for the beans to climb, the beans fix nitrogen in

the soil to benefit the other plants, and the squash spreads along the ground, shading the soil to reduce weeds and conserve moisture.
- Trap Cropping: Some plants are particularly attractive to pests. These can be planted around the perimeter of your garden or near vulnerable crops to draw pests away.
- Beneficial Habitats: Some plants attract beneficial insects, like pollinators or predator insects that control pests. Planting these in your garden can help maintain a healthy ecosystem.
- Intercropping: This involves planting fast-growing crops alongside slower-growing ones. The fast-growing crops are harvested before the slower ones need the space.

Creating Effective Plant Pairs
Certain plant pairs work together exceptionally well. Here are a few examples:
- Tomatoes and Basil: Basil can repel insects harmful to tomatoes and is believed to enhance the flavor of tomatoes.
- Carrots and Onions: The strong smell of onions can deter carrot flies, while carrots can help loosen the soil for the onion's benefit.
- Cucumbers and Nasturtiums: Nasturtiums can repel cucumber beetles and aphids.

Avoiding Incompatible Plant Pairings
Just as some plants work well together, others can interfere with each other's growth. For instance, tomatoes should not be planted with potatoes as they are both susceptible to blight. Similarly, carrots and dill are not good companions because dill can attract carrot flies.

Adapting Companion Planting to Your Garden
Every garden is unique, and companion planting strategies should be adapted to your specific situation. Consider the needs of your plants, the local climate, the size of your garden, and the pests and diseases common to your area.

Experimenting and Observing
Companion planting is as much an art as it is a science. It's important to observe your plants, experiment with different combinations, and learn from your successes and failures.

Remember that pest management is dynamic. Planting marigolds to repel nematodes one year might work well, but the pests could become resistant over time. You need to be flexible and willing to adjust your strategies as needed.

Companion planting is more than just a gardening technique. It's a mindset that views the garden as a diverse, interconnected ecosystem where everything has a role to play. By observing and working with these natural relationships, you can cultivate a more resilient and abundant garden.

In the realm of companion planting, flowers hold a special place. Flowers not only add color and beauty to your garden, but they can also play a crucial role in its health and productivity. Some flowers, like marigolds and nasturtiums, can repel certain pests. Others, like alyssum and cosmos, attract beneficial insects, including pollinators and natural predators of pests. Still others, like comfrey, are deep-rooted "dynamic accumulators" that can bring up nutrients from deep in the soil, making them available to other plants. Incorporating a diverse mix of flowers into your vegetable garden can thus enhance its overall health and productivity. So, as you plan your companion planting strategies, don't forget to include flowers. They're not just pretty faces; they're hardworking members of the garden community.

Preventive measures like row covers

The avoidance of potential problems makes the proposed solutions superfluous. Here are some preventative measures that were created via practice:

The seedlings that were susceptible while forming their root systems were shielded by floating row coverings that shed as the temperatures rose. The fabric barriers prevented flea beetles from feeding on brassicas while allowing adequate light to get through for photosynthesis, so mitigating the danger of overheating.

Alongside transplants that have been toughened off progressively, cold frames retain heat. Acclimatization was fostered by mild microclimates inside as opposed to shock transplanting, which was done directly from the warm environment inside. The vertical sides limit cutworm access, while the bottoms maintain hydration without becoming soaked.

Miniature high tunnels were created by stretching polyethylene or spun bound covers over wire hoops, which sped up the maturation process by extending the growing seasons. The harvests were carried on past the projected endpoints due to the cooling, which also made it more difficult for bugs to discover their spots. Providing aeration while suspending the inflexible constructions that were unnoticed.

Cloches protect individual plants from being nibbled on and can be used into biodiverse plantings that purposefully attract natural predators. Versions made of terracotta and plastic perform the same functions and compliment each other visually, but they are discarded after they are considered safe.

Intercropping is a strategy that is used to discourage tourists from discovering single-crop areas. Companions that either confuse their direction or supply alternative host plants in order to fulfill desires that are directed elsewhere. Marigolds, for instance, drive worms away from tomato plants by emitting a fragrance that is difficult to identify.

Finding a happy medium between human and natural requirements is key to providing abundance for everyone. Respecting nature's delicate co-evolution is the cornerstone of effective stewardship, which is founded on nonviolence. It is best to apply preventatives with discretion in order to avoid dependence.

Listed below are some supplementary pointers concerning precautionary measures such as row covers:

When transplanting seedlings on chilly nights, placing heating caps or mini-hoops over the young plants is recommended. To harden off the plants, remove the covering throughout the day.

Hang pheromone traps that give off aromas to attract pests like cabbage loopers and catch them in the traps before they can cause harm to crops.

Planting insectary flowers, such as dill, fennel, and Queen Anne's lace, which attract beneficial insects in order to organically reduce pests, is highly recommended.

To prevent pests from entering the plant's leaves or roots, you should construct physical barriers around the plants using floating row covers, plastic or wire cylinders.

- Regularly handpick invasive bugs and drop them into soapy water to kill them. Both the imported cabbageworm and the Colorado potato beetle are susceptible to this method.

- Immediately following harvesting, crop debris should be removed so that organisms that cause disease and pests do not have a place to overwinter.

- Rotate annual crops (for example, don't plant brassicas in the same area for two years in a row) in order to break the cycles that pests use to reproduce.

- To prevent illnesses from developing, use drip irrigation and deliver water at the soil level. This will prevent the leaves from being too moist.

- Keep a watchful eye on the crops and solve any problems as soon as possible, preferably before they cause significant harm or become infested.

Book 6 - Seed Starting and Propagation for Ongoing Harvests

Grow lights, heating mats and trays

Indoor gardening offers a world of opportunities, from starting seeds early to growing tropical plants year-round. Key to success in this venture are tools like grow lights, heating mats, and trays. These items replicate or enhance the natural conditions plants need to thrive, allowing you to control the environment and maximize your chances of success.

Understanding Grow Lights
Photosynthesis is the process by which plants convert light into energy. In the outdoor realm, the sun supplies all the light that plants need. Indoors, however, artificial lighting is essential. Grow lights are specially designed to mimic the sun's spectrum of light and to deliver the intensity that plants need for healthy growth.

There are several types of grow lights on the market:
- Fluorescent Lights: These are a popular choice for beginners due to their low cost and wide availability. They're great for seed starting and growing low-light plants.
- LED Lights: More efficient and longer-lasting than fluorescent lights, LED grow lights are an excellent choice for any type of indoor gardening. They also produce less heat, which can be an advantage in a small growing area.
- HID Lights: High-Intensity Discharge (HID) lights are powerful and efficient, making them suitable for growing fruiting and flowering plants. However, they are more expensive and produce more heat than other types of grow lights.

Harnessing the Power of Heating Mats
While light is critical for plant growth, temperature is equally important. Most seeds need warm soil to germinate, and many plants prefer warm roots even after they've sprouted. That's where heating mats come in.

A heating mat is a waterproof, electrically heated pad that goes under your seed trays. It gently warms the soil, promoting faster, more reliable germination. Once your seeds have sprouted, you can continue to use the mat to provide bottom heat until the seedlings are ready to be moved to a cooler environment.

The Role of Trays in Indoor Gardening
Trays serve several purposes in indoor gardening. They contain the soil or other growing medium for your plants, they catch excess water, and they make it easy to move your plants around.

There are different types of trays to consider:
- Seed Starting Trays: These are shallow trays divided into individual cells for starting seeds. They often come with a clear plastic dome to retain humidity.
- Flat Trays: Flat trays without divisions are useful for growing microgreens or for potting up seedlings.
- Trays with Reservoirs: Some trays have a built-in water reservoir and a wicking mat, which can help maintain consistent soil moisture and reduce the frequency of watering.

Putting It All Together
To start seeds indoors, you'll need a grow light, a heating mat, and a seed starting tray. Fill the tray with a seed starting mix, plant your seeds according to the packet instructions, and place the tray on the heating mat under the grow light. Keep the soil moist but not soggy, and wait for the magic to happen.
Once your seedlings have a set of true leaves, you can transplant them into larger pots if necessary. Adjust the height of the grow light to keep it just above the tops of the plants, and gradually reduce the use of the heating mat as the seedlings grow.

Adapting to Your Plants' Needs
Different plants have different needs when it comes to light and temperature. Some plants, like lettuce and herbs, do well with relatively low light and cool temperatures. Others, like tomatoes and peppers, need high light and warm conditions.
Your grow light should be adjustable so you can raise it as your plants grow. The intensity and duration of light that your plants receive can

also be adjusted based on their needs. A timer can be a useful accessory for maintaining a consistent light schedule.

As for temperature, while a heating mat can provide bottom heat, the ambient temperature of your growing area is also important. Most plants prefer a temperature of around 65-75°F, but some tropical plants may need it warmer.

Indoor gardening requires a different set of tools and skills than outdoor gardening, but the rewards are well worth it. With grow lights, heating mats, and trays, you can grow virtually any plant, at any time of year, right in your own home.

In the journey of indoor gardening, humidity plays a pivotal role that often goes unnoticed. Plants lose water through their leaves in a process called transpiration, which is more rapid in dry air. When the air is too dry, plants can lose water faster than their roots can absorb it, leading to symptoms like wilting, brown leaf tips, and slowed growth. Some plants, especially tropical species, also need high humidity to thrive. You can increase humidity around your plants by misting them with water, placing a tray of water near your plants, or using a humidifier. Grouping plants together can also create a more humid microclimate, as the transpiration from each plant will raise the humidity around its neighbors. So, in your indoor gardening adventure, keep indoor gardening offers a world of opportunities, from starting seeds early to growing tropical plants year-round. Key to success in this venture are tools like grow lights, heating mats, and trays. These items replicate or enhance the natural conditions plants need to thrive, allowing you to control the environment and maximize your chances of success.

Understanding Grow Lights

Photosynthesis is the process by which plants convert light into energy. In the outdoor realm, the sun supplies all the light that plants need. Indoors, however, artificial lighting is essential. Grow lights are specially designed to mimic the sun's spectrum of light and to deliver the intensity that plants need for healthy growth.

There are several types of grow lights on the market:
- Fluorescent Lights: These are a popular choice for beginners due to their low cost and wide availability. They're great for seed starting and growing low-light plants.

- LED Lights: More efficient and longer-lasting than fluorescent lights, LED grow lights are an excellent choice for any type of indoor gardening. They also produce less heat, which can be an advantage in a small growing area.
- HID Lights: High-Intensity Discharge (HID) lights are powerful and efficient, making them suitable for growing fruiting and flowering plants. However, they are more expensive and produce more heat than other types of grow lights.

Harnessing the Power of Heating Mats
While light is critical for plant growth, temperature is equally important. Most seeds need warm soil to germinate, and many plants prefer warm roots even after they've sprouted. That's where heating mats come in.
A heating mat is a waterproof, electrically heated pad that goes under your seed trays. It gently warms the soil, promoting faster, more reliable germination. Once your seeds have sprouted, you can continue to use the mat to provide bottom heat until the seedlings are ready to be moved to a cooler environment.

The Role of Trays in Indoor Gardening
Trays serve several purposes in indoor gardening. They contain the soil or other growing medium for your plants, they catch excess water, and they make it easy to move your plants around.

There are different types of trays to consider:
- Seed Starting Trays: These are shallow trays divided into individual cells for starting seeds. They often come with a clear plastic dome to retain humidity.
- Flat Trays: Flat trays without divisions are useful for growing microgreens or for potting up seedlings.
- Trays with Reservoirs: Some trays have a built-in water reservoir and a wicking mat, which can help maintain consistent soil moisture and reduce the frequency of watering.

Putting It All Together
To start seeds indoors, you'll need a grow light, a heating mat, and a seed starting tray. Fill the tray with a seed starting mix, plant your seeds according to the packet instructions, and place the tray on the

heating mat under the grow light. Keep the soil moist but not soggy, and wait for the magic to happen.

Once your seedlings have a set of true leaves, you can transplant them into larger pots if necessary. Adjust the height of the grow light to keep it just above the tops of the plants, and gradually reduce the use of the heating mat as the seedlings grow.

Adapting to Your Plants' Needs

Different plants have different needs when it comes to light and temperature. Some plants, like lettuce and herbs, do well with relatively low light and cool temperatures. Others, like tomatoes and peppers, need high light and warm conditions.

Your grow light should be adjustable so you can raise it as your plants grow. The intensity and duration of light that your plants receive can also be adjusted based on their needs. A timer can be a useful accessory for maintaining a consistent light schedule.

As for temperature, while a heating mat can provide bottom heat, the ambient temperature of your growing area is also important. Most plants prefer a temperature of around 65-75°F, but some tropical plants may need it warmer.

Indoor gardening requires a different set of tools and skills than outdoor gardening, but the rewards are well worth it. With grow lights, heating mats, and trays, you can grow virtually any plant, at any time of year, right in your own home.

In the journey of indoor gardening, humidity plays a pivotal role that often goes unnoticed. Plants lose water through their leaves in a process called transpiration, which is more rapid in dry air. When the air is too dry, plants can lose water faster than their roots can absorb it, leading to symptoms like wilting, brown leaf tips, and slowed growth. Some plants, especially tropical species, also need high humidity to thrive. You can increase humidity around your plants by misting them with water, placing a tray of water near your plants, or using a humidifier. Grouping plants together can also create a more humid microclimate, as the transpiration from each plant will raise the humidity around its neighbors.

Timing seed starts for continuous yields

However, lessons taught discipline, which prolonged the harvest rhythms despite the impatience that encouraged hurrying the transplants. A meticulous planting schedule maximizes growth areas for repeated sowings, which in turn caters to diversity:

Carrots, radishes, and lettuce grow immediately following the warming of the soil, which is the first step in the cultivation of cool-weather crops for spring consumption. Place seed envelopes indoors to hasten the process of hardening off, as opposed to placing them outdoors too soon, when they would experience slow development. The more cold-resistant varieties, such as kale, spinach, and chard, are started inside around six weeks before the last spring frosts. This allows the plants to acclimatize and improve their constitutions. Once temperatures have stabilized, stronger transplants can be used.

Tomatoes, peppers, and eggplants need to be started under lights eight weeks before they are ready to be transplanted so that the sun can fortify the top growth and make the plant more resistant. Plantings should be staggered to provide longer cropping.

Once the soil has reached the proper temperature for germination, heat-loving plants like beans, squash, and cucumbers can be directly seeded two months before the projected start of summer. Solarization performed in advance sterilizes the land.

The continuity of the developing process is maintained by the use of succession sowing. When one patch is finished producing, another begins growing in its place to provide a steady supply of ripe goods to satisfy customers throughout the season. The coordination of efforts requires intelligent preparation.

The ability to time the photoperiodic reactions of bulbs and perennials keeps the interest level high throughout the year. Experimentation helps perfect procedures until a skilled ballerina can sustain flow in a way that is as naturally everlasting as rivers and stars.

The following are some more suggestions on the time of seed starts in order to maintain continuous yields:

- Make use of a seed starting mix that has been specially prepared to provide enough drainage and nourishment to seedlings. Garden soil that could be infected with illness should not be used.

- A day should consist of between 18 and 24 hours of warm, intense light to promote consistent and rapid development. The use of fluorescent light bulbs is effective.

- A week spent acclimating seedlings to the light, wind, and cooler temperatures of the outdoors before transplanting them prepares them for their new environment.

- Instead of planting all of your seeds at once, stagger them so that your harvest will take place over a period of two to four weeks.

- The season can be stretched even further by selecting cultivars that mature at different times (for example, tomatoes that mature in 65-80 days).

- In springs that are more likely to be affected by frost, it is best to begin additional seedlings indoors as a hedge against the possibility of weather-related setbacks.
- To ensure a constant supply of leafy greens, such as lettuce and kale, you should sow new seeds at intervals of around two to three weeks.

- Keep an eye on the crop calendars that are specific to your planting zone, and make adjustments to your schedules depending on the typical first and latest frost dates.

- Keep a record of the outcomes from each year so that you may improve your procedures and achieve earlier, more dependable, and more fruitful harvests.

Hardening off and transplanting methods

The journey of a seedling, from the safety of its indoor nursery to the expansive, unpredictable outdoors, is an undeniably exciting one. This transition, known as hardening off, is a crucial step in the plant's life and requires careful techniques to ensure survival and growth. Successful hardening off, followed by effective transplanting methods, can set your young plants up for a thriving life in the garden.

Understanding Hardening Off
Hardening off is a process that gradually acclimates indoor-grown seedlings to outdoor conditions. It typically involves exposing the seedlings to outdoor weather gradually over a period of one to two

weeks before transplanting them into the garden. The process helps the seedlings adjust to sunlight, wind, and temperature fluctuations, reducing the risk of transplant shock.

Here's a step-by-step guide on how to harden off your plants:
1. Start Gradually: Begin by placing your seedlings outdoors in a shaded, sheltered location for just an hour or two. Avoid direct sun and strong winds during the first few days.

2. Increase Exposure Time: Gradually increase the amount of time your seedlings spend outside each day. Add a couple of hours to their outdoor time every day until they can stay outdoors for a full 24 hours.

3. Introduce Sunlight and Wind: Once your seedlings are comfortable with extended outdoor time, you can start introducing them to sunlight and wind. Start with morning sun which is gentler than afternoon sun, and increase their exposure over several days.

4. Monitor Weather Conditions: Keep a close eye on the weather. If temperatures dip below 50 degrees Fahrenheit (10 degrees Celsius), or if there's a risk of frost, bring your seedlings back inside.

5. Keep Up with Watering: Seedlings dry out faster outdoors, so be sure to keep up with watering. However, avoid overwatering as this can lead to root rot or fungal diseases.

After completing the hardening off process, your seedlings would be ready for transplanting.

Mastering the Art of Transplanting
Transplanting is the process of moving a plant from one growing environment to another. For seedlings, this often means moving from a small seed tray to a larger pot or directly into the garden. Proper transplanting techniques can minimize stress and set your plants up for success.
Here are some steps to follow when transplanting your seedlings:

1. Choose the Right Time: The best time to transplant is on a cloudy day or in the early morning or late evening. This reduces the chance of the seedlings wilting under the harsh sunlight.

2. Prepare the New Location: If transplanting into the garden, dig a hole that's wide and deep enough to accommodate the seedling's roots. If you're moving the seedling to a larger pot, make sure it has plenty of fresh potting soil.

3. Remove the Seedling Carefully: Hold the stem of the seedling between your fingers and turn the pot upside down, gently tapping until the plant and its root ball come out. Avoid pulling on the stem, as this can damage the plant.

4. Place the Seedling in Its New Home: Place the seedling in the hole or pot, ensuring the top of the root ball is level with the soil surface. Fill in around the root ball with soil, pressing gently to remove air pockets.

5. Water Thoroughly: Water the seedling immediately after transplanting. This helps settle the soil and reduces transplant shock.

6. Monitor Your Transplanted Seedlings: Keep an eye on your plants for a few weeks after transplanting. They may wilt initially as they adjust to their new environment, but should perk up with proper care.

It's also worth noting that not all plants respond well to transplanting. Some, like carrots and radishes, prefer to be sown directly where they will grow to maturity. Always check the seed packet or plant tag for specific planting instructions.

A Word on Succession Planting
One advantage of starting seeds indoors and transplanting them outdoors is the opportunity for succession planting. This is the practice of planting crops in staggered waves to ensure a continuous harvest throughout the growing season. By starting a new batch of seeds indoors every two to three weeks, you can have a steady stream of seedlings ready to transplant whenever a space opens up in your garden.

Succession planting requires good timing and organization, but it can greatly increase your yield and extend your harvest season. It works well with many crops, including lettuce, radishes, and beans.

In essence, the journey from seed to mature plant is a delicate dance that requires patience, skills, and knowledge. By understanding and implementing the crucial steps of hardening off and transplanting, you can ensure your seedlings grow into strong, healthy, and productive plants. And with the added strategy of succession planting, your garden can provide a bounty of fresh produce throughout the entire growing season.

Saving seeds from your best plants

Maintaining valued characteristics is essential to keeping hard-won successes, and doing so through intentional selection helps to eliminate unpredictability. The following methods, which I devised, guarantee reliability:

The process of hybridization creates a wider variety of attractive pairings. The use of hand pollination allows for the separation of desired characteristics, the prevention of cross-contamination, and the thorough labeling required for the monitoring of progeny. Excellence may be identified through observation, which then leads to the development of cultivars.

The trueness of open-pollinated types may be consistently reproduced by removing weaker specimens prior to flowering and making selective cuts. Pollen may be collected without pollutants by using bags. The mature seeds are simplest to collect from green umbels as opposed to the finicky tomatoes.

To maintain viability, storage must be done in conditions of low heat and humidity. Labeling seeds using paper envelopes or glassine bags prevents them from inhaling ethylene gas, which speeds up the loss of germination. Under ideal conditions, dormancy can be prolonged by vacuum sealing for several decades.

Testing conducted shortly after extraction provides an estimate of lifespans. The planting percentage checks the viability of the crop, helping to prevent wasted nursery space. Jars that have been hermetically sealed and placed under refrigeration provide protection for very sensitive newly matured seeds.

The records include information on the lineage as well as the locality adapting kinds. Microclimates encourage the evolution of strains that are particularly adapted to their environment. The preservation of regional specialization helps to maintain isolation and prevents different landraces from being diluted by hybridization.

Sharing helps increase biodiversity, which in turn improves the food security of the community. collaboration between neighbors helps to propagate experimentation, which, in turn, inspires improvements to communities through fostering collaboration and improvisation. The cultivation of togetherness brings forth the riches that nature intended for everybody.

Additional helpful hints for storing seeds from your most productive plants are as follows:
- It is best to wait until the seeds have reached their full maturity on the plant before harvesting them. This provides the highest possible level of viability.

- To prevent any harm, carefully remove the seeds from the dried seed heads or pods. On labels, the source plant and the date should be noted.

- To prevent problems in the crops of the future from being perpetuated, you should only save the seeds from disease-resistant plants.

- It is important to maintain genetic isolation by maintaining adequate distance between different types of cross-pollinating plants.

- In order to prevent mold and fungus from growing on stored seeds, it is important to completely dry them out before putting them away.

- Place the seeds of biennials and other short-lived perennials in airtight containers and place them in the refrigerator.

- To evaluate the performance of seeds over a period of years, keep complete records on seed attributes, circumstances, yields, and other relevant information.

Book 7 - Designing Your Layout for Year-Round Production

Arranging for crop rotation

Crop rotation, a practice as ancient as agriculture itself, holds the key to healthy and productive farming. This age-old method, used by our farming ancestors, has profound benefits. It bolsters soil fertility, curbs pests and diseases, and promotes bountiful harvests. To a novice farmer or gardener, arranging for crop rotation may seem like a complex task, but it need not be. Let's unravel the mystery of crop rotation and learn how to put it into practice.

The Importance of Crop Rotation
Crop rotation is the practice of growing different crops in the same area over sequential seasons. The aim is to improve soil health, increase crop yield, and reduce pest and disease problems. The benefits of this practice are numerous and include:

- Soil Fertility Enhancement: Different crops have varied nutrient requirements. By rotating crops, you can prevent the depletion of specific nutrients and help maintain soil fertility.
- Pest and Disease Control: Pests and diseases often target specific plant families. By changing the crops each season, you can disrupt the life cycles of these pests and diseases, reducing their populations.
- Improved Crop Yield: Healthier soil and fewer pests and diseases often lead to an increase in crop yield.
- Promotion of Biodiversity: Crop rotation encourages a diverse range of organisms in the soil, contributing to a healthier ecosystem.

Planning Your Crop Rotation
Creating a crop rotation plan requires some knowledge of the crops you intend to grow. Here are key steps to help you design a successful crop rotation plan:
1. Know Your Crops: Get familiar with the families your crops belong to. Plants in the same family are often susceptible to similar pests and diseases and have similar nutrient needs.

2. Divide Your Garden into Sections: You will rotate crops between these sections each year.
3. Keep Records: Document what you plant in each section each year. This record-keeping will guide your rotation in the future.

A Simple Four-Year Crop Rotation Plan
A four-year rotation plan is common and manageable for many gardeners. Here is a basic framework for such a plan:

- Year 1: Plant legumes, such as beans and peas. These plants fix nitrogen in the soil, improving its fertility.
- Year 2: Plant fruiting crops like tomatoes, peppers, or cucumbers. These plants are heavy feeders and will benefit from the extra nitrogen.
- Year 3: Plant root vegetables such as potatoes, carrots, and beets. These plants prefer less nitrogen but require a well-aerated soil structure.
- Year 4: Plant leafy greens like lettuce, spinach, and kale. These plants can thrive even when the nutrient levels are relatively lower.
Remember, this is just a basic framework and your crop rotation plan may vary based on your specific circumstances and preferences.

Adapting and Refining Your Plan
Crop rotation plans are not set in stone. As you gain experience, you can adapt and refine your plan based on your observations and specific needs. For instance, if you notice a particular pest problem, you might opt to leave a section fallow or plant a pest-resistant cover crop. The key is to remain flexible and responsive to your garden's needs.
It's also worth noting that crop rotation is just one tool in a gardener's toolbox. It should be used in conjunction with other good practices like composting, mulching, and intercropping for the best results.
The concept of companion planting can also play a crucial role in your crop rotation plan. Companion plants are crops that benefit each other when planted together. For instance, corn provides a natural trellis for beans, while beans fix nitrogen in the soil that corn can use. By incorporating companion planting into your crop rotation plan, you can further enhance the benefits of both practices.

Furthermore, cover crops can be an essential part of your crop rotation plan. These plants are grown primarily to manage soil erosion, soil fertility, soil quality, water, weeds, pests, diseases, biodiversity and wildlife in an ecosystem. Incorporating cover crops like clover or rye can improve soil structure, add nutrients, and suppress weeds.

In essence, the practice of crop rotation is a dynamic dance with nature, respecting the natural cycles and uniqueness of each plant. The more we understand and work in harmony with these natural processes, the more fruitful our gardens become. Crop rotation, combined with companion planting and the use of cover crops, is an effective strategy for a healthy, productive garden.

Maximizing sun throughout the seasons

Productivity may be significantly increased by making smart use of sunlight. Experimentation in the early stages refined orientation: Rows running north to south ensured that the sun's rays entered the canopy at an angle that was perpendicular over the course of the day. In contrast to the crowded east-west lanes, which tend to dominate one side during peak hours and leave the others in the shadows, alleyways that are wider and can be entered from either direction are more convenient for caretaking.

Mounding that is concave helps to retain moisture while at the same time allowing light to penetrate more evenly than flatbeds, which tend to concentrate damp places that get boggy. In areas where prolonged dampening fostered decay, raised ridges helped speed drainage.

Tal lectors, like as sunflowers, erected southerly direct sunlight, which scatters diffusely and benefits neighboring areas when the sun is at a lower angle in the afternoon. The micro herds that formed from the decomposition of their leaves later enhanced the soil.

Dwarf fruit trees can be trained to grow in a flat pattern against struts running north to south, maximizing the amount of sunlight that reaches each branch and making the most of limited space. Easy-to-carry out pruning level spiking while simultaneously permitting cross winds.

Season extenders such as low hoop tunnels shielded fragile transplants that were about to wither exposed but were nevertheless removed in the summer to prevent overheating permitted the prolonging of both ends of the season and increased availability. Experimentation, research, and efforts toward sustainability. Complementarity, not rivalry, is what allows biodiversity to flourish. Integration rather than segregation synergizes productivity, rather than segregating it, and privileges the process over the momentary yield. Balanced wisdom and values consistently outperforming short-term gains that eventually run out of steam.

Extra pointers to help you get the most out of your solar exposure during the growth seasons:

Use shade cloth hung from flexible frames to provide protection from the intense midday heat for delicate crops like lettuce without obstructing the light that the plants need.

To prevent the plants in the garden beds from becoming shaded, plant tall crops on the north side of the bed and low crops on the south side.

- Plant in succession so that there are no gaps between harvests and when fresh sowings are ready to make use of the area when it becomes available.

- If you have limited room, you should position vegetable rows east-west rather than north-south to ensure that each plant receives an equal amount of sunlight.

- Plant annual crops such as radishes and spinach in areas where the sun's rays will be at a different angle in the future to provide place for later plantings.

- Planting dates should be staggered for heat-loving crops so that the harvest window can be extended by a few weeks as the sun's angle rises higher in the sky.

Because the soil quality will certainly change throughout the course of the growing season inside the garden, it is important to keep an eye on it and rotate the crops in order to redistribute the fertility.

When planning where to place your crops as the season develops, you may want to take into consideration mobile constructions such as little hoop homes on wheels.

When staggered and positioned correctly, unoccupied times are eliminated and continuous collection of the sun's energy is achieved.

Strategies for small spaces

As urbanization continues to grow, many of us find ourselves with limited space to indulge our green thumbs. But limited space should not curb your gardening ambitions. With a bit of creativity and strategic planning, you can transform even the smallest of spaces into a lush, productive garden. Whether you have a small yard, a balcony, or just a sunny windowsill, there are strategies to make the most of your available space.

Embracing Vertical Gardening
One of the most efficient ways to maximize gardening prospects in small spaces is by growing upwards. Vertical gardening not only saves space but also adds an aesthetic element to your garden or balcony. Here are some ways to create a vertical garden:
- Trellises and Supports: Use trellises, cages, stakes, or netting to support climbing plants like tomatoes, cucumbers, beans, and peas.
- Hanging Baskets: Great for growing a variety of herbs, small vegetables, and flowering plants.
- Wall Planters: Attach planters to walls or fences to grow herbs, succulents, or ornamental plants.
- Tower Planters: These are specially designed for vertical growth and are perfect for a variety of crops, including strawberries, lettuce, and herbs.

Using Containers Effectively
Container gardening is another excellent solution for small spaces. Almost any plant can be grown in a container, provided it's large enough to accommodate the plant's growth. Here are some tips for successful container gardening:
- Choose the Right Container: Ensure it's the right size for your plant and it has proper drainage. Remember, it's easier to grow plants in larger containers than small ones because the soil in larger containers retains moisture longer.
- Use Quality Soil: Use a high-quality potting mix that provides proper drainage and nutrient retention.

- Water and Fertilize Regularly: Containers need more frequent watering and fertilizing than plants in the ground.

Selecting Suitable Plants
Choosing the right plants can make a big difference in small space gardening. Opti for plants that naturally stay small or dwarf varieties of larger plants. Some plants, like tomatoes, peppers, and eggplants, have specifically been bred for container growth and are perfect for small space gardens.

Interplanting and Succession Planting
Interplanting involves growing two or more types of plants together in the same space to make the most of available resources. For example, you could plant a fast-growing crop like lettuce alongside a slower-growing crop like tomatoes. By the time the tomatoes need more space, the lettuce will have been harvested.
Succession planting is another great strategy for small spaces. This involves planting a new crop as soon as the previous crop is harvested. This way, you get multiple harvests from the same space.

Creating Microclimates
Understanding and using microclimates can help you make the most of your small garden. Different areas of your garden, no matter how small, will have different microclimates. You can use these to grow a wider variety of plants. For example, a wall might reflect heat and create a warm microclimate perfect for heat-loving plants. On the other hand, a shady corner could be great for shade-loving plants.

Utilizing Indoor Spaces
Don't forget about your indoor spaces. Windowsills, sunny countertops, and even walls can be turned into productive growing areas. Many herbs, leafy greens, and even some fruiting plants like peppers and tomatoes can be grown successfully indoors with enough light.

Embracing Hydroponics
Hydroponics is a method of growing plants in nutrient-rich water instead of soil. Hydroponic systems can be very space-efficient, making them ideal for small space gardening. With hydroponics, you

can grow a wide variety of crops, including herbs, leafy greens, and fruiting plants.

In essence, gardening in small spaces doesn't mean you have to limit your creativity or productivity. In fact, it might just be the catalyst for developing innovative gardening solutions and strategies. With the right approach, you can turn your limited space into a bountiful garden.

Remember, the beauty of gardening lies not in the size of the garden but in the joy it brings. Even the smallest garden can offer an oasis of calm and a sense of accomplishment. So, embrace your small space, roll up your sleeves, and start planting. Your dream garden is just a few strategic steps away.

Incorporating vertical growing

Gains in productivity motivate evaluation on an ongoing basis, which in turn leads to investigation above soils:

Vines that have fruited are kept above the ground by trellises, which preserve ventilation and ward off infections. The spaces in between the beds are elegantly decorated with cucumber and melon vines, along with a few bean plants.

Instead of concentrating their weight on the soil and causing it to contract, cages allow indeterminate tomato plants to mature in stages throughout the summer. The use of stakes makes protection and harvesting easier.

Grape clusters are kept separate and ripening consistently, undamaged, and uncluttered beneath nets that are strung so that overwintering cuttings may be jostled upward, conserving terrestrial space.

The espalier tree's appendage and branch structure prevent russet figs and pears from growing against buildings, guiding growth to flat surfaces, and making the most of restricted spatial dimensions in urban situations. Levels of pruning allow for orderly harvests.

Cherries grown on serpentine cordons are able to produce longer fruiting spans, carry more laterals, and produce fruit over a longer period of time.

Layering that is done with consideration incorporates many stores of stacking functions to maximize the effectiveness of recording inputs. Perennial understories, such as asparagus, provide food for annual canopies above, which helps the ecosystem to remain fertile. Mindsets that are synergistic generate plenty despite limits.

Expansive thoughts promote future discoveries, boosting the possibility for sustainability, and getting closer to the arduous summit of productivity. Creative Effort simple technological advancement, while _wisdom_ directs application in the service of community well-being.

The following are some more suggestions for adopting approaches for vertical growing:

- Pole bean variants, which are more prolific than bush bean varieties, should be grown using bamboo, wooden posts, or wire cages.

- Train cucumbers and winter squash to grow up parallel strings that are tied to fences or other structures to improve air circulation.

In order to achieve the highest possible yield, interweave twine or netting between vine support posts that are tightly spaced apart.

- To ensure a continuous harvest, interplant lettuce, herbs, or flowers that mature quickly in the space between tomato cages.

- Trellising and stakes should be adjusted to accommodate the growth patterns of both determinate and indeterminate kinds.

You might want to think about cultivating berries in a vertical fashion by using hanging baskets or raised beds lined with plastic or woven mesh.

Allow trailing plants the space they need to grow by planting them in an arch or tepee form and securing them with rope.
When you have limited room, you may plant edibles on the railings of balconies, along walls, or along the boundaries of gardens by using solid brackets.
Ensure that the stability of the support systems is maintained as the fruit matures to reduce the risk of harm from either wind or weight.

Book 8 - Maintaining Optimal Growing Conditions

Temperature, light and ventilation management

Cultivating a thriving indoor garden or greenhouse doesn't just happen by chance. It requires a careful balance of key elements: temperature, light, and ventilation. By managing these three aspects, you can create an optimal environment for your plants to flourish. Whether you're growing delicate orchids or hearty tomatoes, understanding and controlling these factors are crucial. So, let's dive into each one and explore how they work together to ensure a healthy, productive growing space.

Temperature: The Heat of the Matter
Temperature plays a pivotal role in plant growth. It affects germination, photosynthesis, transpiration, and the overall metabolism of the plant. Here's how to manage it:

- Understand Your Plants' Needs: Different plants have different temperature requirements. Research your plants to learn their optimal temperature range. For instance, tropical plants prefer warmer temperatures, while many herbs prefer cooler conditions.

- Use a Thermostat: A thermostat can be a gardener's best friend. It allows you to maintain a consistent temperature, which is vital for plant health.

- Use Heaters or Coolers if Necessary: If your indoor garden or greenhouse is too cold, you may need to use a heater. Conversely, if it's too hot, a cooler may be necessary.

Light: Let There Be Light
Light is essential for photosynthesis, the process by which plants convert light energy into chemical energy to fuel their growth. Here's how to manage it:

- Know the Light Requirements: Different plants require different amounts of light. Some plants need full sun, while others do well in partial shade. Understand what each plant needs and position them accordingly.

- Use Artificial Lights: In indoor settings, natural light might be insufficient. In such cases, artificial lights like LED grow lights can supplement or replace natural light.

- Control Light Exposure: Use timers to regulate light exposure. Most plants need a period of darkness each day, just as they would get in nature.

Ventilation: The Breath of Fresh Air
Proper ventilation is crucial for the health of indoor and greenhouse plants. It helps control temperature and humidity, prevents the buildup of fungal diseases, and strengthens plants by causing them to move, much like they would in a breeze outdoors. Here's how to manage it:

- Ensure Good Airflow: Use fans to circulate air. This is particularly important in greenhouses or indoor gardens where natural airflow might be limited.

- Create Openings: If possible, create openings or vents in your indoor or greenhouse space that can be opened or closed as needed.

- Be Mindful of Humidity: Some plants thrive in humid conditions while others prefer less humidity. Use a hygrometer to measure humidity levels and adjust your ventilation accordingly.

Bringing It All Together: The Harmony of Elements
Managing temperature, light, and ventilation in your indoor garden or greenhouse is a balancing act. Each element influences the others. For example, too much light can raise the temperature and lower humidity, while poor ventilation can lead to high humidity and temperature fluctuations.

Use technology to your advantage. Tools like digital thermostats, programmable light timers, and automated ventilation systems can help you maintain the optimal environment for your plants. But remember, observation is just as important. Pay attention to your plants; they'll often show signs if they're not happy. Wilting, yellowing leaves, or slow growth can all be signs that your temperature, light, or ventilation isn't quite right.

In the end, the goal of managing these elements is to mimic the conditions your plants would experience in their natural habitats as closely as possible. And while it might seem like a challenging task, with a bit of practice and patience, you'll soon become adept at creating the perfect indoor or greenhouse garden oasis.

One overlooked technique in managing these elements is the practice of grouping plants with similar needs together. This strategy, known as "zoning", allows you to create microclimates within your garden or greenhouse. For example, you could group together plants that prefer lower light and higher humidity in one area, and those that need full light and lower humidity in another. By zoning your plants, you can provide more precise care, leading to healthier, happier plants. This practice not only makes your gardening more efficient but also helps create a visually pleasing arrangement. So, as you manage temperature, light, and ventilation, consider zoning as an additional tool in your gardening strategy toolbox.

Caring for plants in extreme weather

Although nature finally demonstrates flawless resilience, preparation softens the impacts caused by extremes. Strategies that are able to withstand storms:

Compassion recognizes the cyclical nature of vulnerability. In the fall, woody perennials get a boost before the first hard frost, while fragile bulbs are encouraged to start their subterranean vegetation. Having patience enables adaptation to take place on nature's timetable.

Row covers insulate annuals, which helps to minimize spring setbacks for plants whose origins lay mostly inside. Protecting transplants from the harshness of the external environment while also allowing photosynthesis behind cloth light filters.

Supported by stakes Tomatoes that have reached their full maturity have developed a lanky appearance as a result of the summer's heat and wind. Developed root systems that act as an anchor despite the fact that the tresses are becoming thicker every day.

Sheltered microclimates often contain overflowing planters and welcome wildlife in abundance even during dry spells. Refugees between buildings never run dry and always serve to refresh the surrounding community.

Porosity ventilates present conditions comfortably, regardless of whether they are indoors or outdoors, conserves moisture, stays dry during rain, and lacks only sun exposure directly required. Flexibility is of benefit to everyone.

Having an understanding of natural cycles can help avoid needless mechanical progress being made. Revelry nature awakens watchful eyes to watchful appreciation of her perfect orchestration stewarding still centuries of history.

Additional suggestions for the care of plants during harsh weather conditions are as follows:

During periods of extreme heat or cold, frost- or heat-sensitive crops should be protected with shade cloth or temporary coverings.

During times of drought, it is more important to water deeply and rarely in order to promote deep root development rather than surface soaking.

It is important to apply a thick layer of mulch around plants in order to avoid moisture loss and the growth of weeds.

Remove storm-damaged branches after the storm, but hold off on any trimming until the new growth appears.

Before the arrival of strong gusts, stake or tie the vines securely so they won't become tangled or snap.

Wrapping pipes with insulation or keeping valves slightly ajar can prevent water from freezing and bursting if they are exposed to the elements.

To protect containers from breaking caused by the cycle of freezing and thawing, bring them under cover or cover them with a piece of plastic.

To prevent damage from flooding, prepare the soil drainage in advance by building berms, swales, or gravel trenches.

Scout the area following severe weather for any symptoms of infectious diseases or insect infestations that have been aggravated by the stress.

Adjust your expectations in light of the fact that the occasional excesses caused by nature cannot always be managed or avoided.

Trellising, staking and pruning over time

The art of gardening involves much more than just planting seeds and watching them grow. To optimize plant health and productivity, especially in limited spaces, trellising, staking, and pruning are essential techniques for gardeners to master. These practices not only support plant growth but also facilitate better airflow, reduce disease, and can enhance yield. So, let's explore these techniques and understand how they can be effectively employed over time.

Trellising: Up We Go
Trellising is a method of training plants to grow upward, which is especially useful for vining plants like tomatoes, cucumbers, and peas. Here are key points to consider when implementing trellising:

- Choose the Right Trellis: Trellises come in many designs, from simple stakes with string to elaborate metal or wood structures. Select one that suits your space, budget, and the type of plant you're growing.

- Timing: Install your trellis at the time of planting to avoid disturbing the roots later.

- Training: Gently weave or tie the plant to the trellis as it grows. Be careful not to damage the plant in the process.

Staking: Providing Support
Staking involves inserting a stake into the ground next to the plant and tying the plant to the stake as it grows. It's commonly used for tall, single-stemmed plants like tomatoes and peppers. Here's how to do it:

- Stake Selection: Stakes should be sturdy and long enough for your plant's full-grown height. Bamboo, wood, or metal stakes are commonly used.

- Placement: Place the stake about 4 inches away from the plant to avoid damaging the roots.

- Tying: Use a soft material like cloth or plant tape to tie the plant to the stake. Don't tie it too tight; the plant needs some room to grow.

Pruning: A Cut Above
Pruning involves removing certain parts of a plant to improve its shape, encourage growth, or remove dead or diseased material. Here's how to prune effectively:

- Understand Your Plant: Some plants benefit from frequent pruning, while others do not. Research your plant's pruning needs before getting started.

- Tools: Use a sharp, clean pair of pruning shears to make clean cuts and prevent disease.

- Timing: Most plants are best pruned in late winter or early spring, but timing can vary based on the type of plant and the reason for pruning.

- Technique: When pruning, make your cut at a 45-degree angle about 1/4 inch above a bud that is facing the outside of the plant. This will help the plant grow in a desirable shape.

The Art of Patience: Watching Your Garden Grow
Trellising, staking, and pruning are not one-time tasks. They require regular attention and adjustment as your plants grow. Be patient and observe your plants closely. As you gain experience, you'll become more adept at recognizing when and how to intervene.
In your gardening journey, you'll likely encounter moments of uncertainty. Remember, it's okay to make mistakes. Each mistake is a learning opportunity that will make you a better gardener in the long run. So, take the time to understand your plants, provide them with the support they need, and intervene with pruning when necessary. One aspect that often gets overlooked in the discussion of trellising, staking, and pruning is the opportunity these techniques provide to engage with your plants. Each interaction offers a chance to observe your plants closely. You'll notice if pests are starting to invade, if a disease is taking hold, or if a plant is not thriving for some reason. These techniques, therefore, not only support the growth of your plants but also enhance your own growth as a gardener. They deepen your relationship with your plants and improve your ability to care for them effectively. This intimate connection with your garden is one of the most rewarding aspects of gardening. So, as you trellis, stake, and prune, remember that you're not just cultivating plants; you're cultivating a deeper understanding and appreciation of the wonders of nature.

Ensuring excellent flavor and nutrients

However, concerns about my health were the impetus behind my motivations. Unassuming components provide tremendous nourishment:

Tomato stir-fries with basil offer a level of intricacy that is unmatched by store-bought versions while requiring only a small amount of preparation. The elevation of quality enlightens palates while simultaneously enveloping families in their heritage.

Even broths that aren't particularly flavorful can be elevated to a higher level with the addition of "powerhouses" like dark leafy greens ground into pesto. This makes mineral density more accessible. Experiments are what make exploring exciting.

Fermentation results in the natural cultivation of probiotics, while also keeping bounty for the winter months and providing nourishment that is incomparable to that provided by lifeless alternatives while maintaining stability without the need of chemical preservatives.

Taking a Look At guided cultivar selection that speaks to the intricacies of the terroir refined taste profiles that are appealing, yet are excessively full and lacking in nourishment. Different levels of connoisseurship The practice of kindness trains one to exercise restraint.

The practice of mindfulness was maintained throughout the harvest, which contributed to the advancement of wellness in a democratic manner for all those who were seeking contentment. Nature offers abundantly without the need for labor or transaction, and it is as delightfully varied as sunshine.

The following are some extra suggestions that will help you get the most out of your homegrown produce in terms of flavor and nutrition:

For the best flavor, go with heritage and open-pollinated kinds that have been carefully chosen over the years by experienced farmers.

If you want the sweetest fruits and vegetables and the best possible growth of their nutrients, you should let them fully mature on the plant.

Refrigerate the produce as quickly as possible after it has been picked to preserve its quality as well as the amounts of nutrients it contains.

Preserve the abundance of the season by preserving, drying, or fermenting it so that you may enjoy the culinary payoffs long after the crops have passed their prime.

To get a wide variety of vitamins, minerals, antioxidants, and phytonutrients, eat a variety of different kinds of vegetables and fruits at each meal.

Instead of adding salt or oil, use fresh herbs to bring out the tastes and enhance the nutritional value of everything from salads to entrees.

Book 9 - Preserving and Storing Your Harvest Bounty

Freezing, canning, drying and cold storage

The fruits of your gardening labor are ripe and ready. But what if there's more than you can eat? Or what if you're looking forward to those juicy tomatoes or crisp apples when winter comes? Preserving your harvest through freezing, canning, drying, and cold storage is the answer. These methods not only extend the shelf life of your produce but also lock in the flavor and nutritional value. Let's explore these techniques and how best to apply them.

Freezing: The Cold Keeper
Freezing is one of the simplest ways to preserve your fruits and vegetables. It slows down the enzyme activity that causes food to spoil.

- Preparation: Clean your produce thoroughly. Some vegetables benefit from blanching (briefly boiling) before freezing.

- Storage: Use airtight containers or freezer bags. Remove as much air as possible to prevent freezer burn.

- Organization: Label each package with the contents and date. Try to use your oldest items first to ensure quality.

Canning: Preserving in a Jar
Canning involves sealing food in jars and heating them to kill microorganisms that cause spoilage. It's ideal for preserving a variety of fruits, vegetables, and even sauces.

- Sterilization: Sterilize your jars, lids, and rings by boiling them before use.

- Packing: Pack your produce into jars, leaving the recommended headspace. Add any necessary liquids like syrup or brine.

- Processing: Process the jars in a water bath or pressure canner, depending on the food.

- Storage: Once cooled, check the seals. Store in a cool, dark place.

Drying: The Ancient Art
Drying removes the water that bacteria, yeast, and mold need to grow. It's a great method for preserving herbs, fruits, and vegetables.

- Preparation: Clean and cut your produce into evenly sized pieces.

- Drying: Use an oven, dehydrator, or natural sun drying, depending on the food and your climate.

- Storage: Store dried foods in airtight containers in a cool, dark place.

Cold Storage: Nature's Refrigerator
Cold storage uses cool, humid conditions to prolong the life of certain fruits and vegetables. It's ideal for root vegetables, apples, and pears.

- Selection: Only store produce that's in good condition. One bad apple can indeed spoil the whole bunch!

- Packaging: Pack your produce in boxes, bins, or bags that allow for airflow.

- Environment: Store in a cool (32-40°F / 0-4°C), humid (80-95% relative humidity) environment.

Each of these methods has its own benefits and is suitable for different types of produce. It's worth experimenting to find which methods you prefer. Just remember, safety is paramount. Always adhere to recommended guidelines to ensure your preserved foods are safe to eat.

Preserving your harvest not only provides you with fresh, homegrown produce year-round, but it also connects you with the cycles of nature and the rhythm of the seasons. As you freeze the surplus from your summer harvest, can your homemade tomato sauce, dry the herbs from your garden, or store apples for a mid-winter treat, you're participating in an age-old tradition of sustainability and self-reliance. These preservation techniques not only extend the life of your food but also deepen your relationship with the food you grow and eat.

One intriguing aspect of preserving food is the potential it holds for creativity. While the processes of freezing, canning, drying, and cold storage follow certain scientific principles for safety and effectiveness, within those parameters, there's ample room for experimentation. You might find yourself developing unique spice blends for the pickles you're canning, or creating fruit leathers with surprising flavor combinations. Perhaps you'll perfect the art of storing different apple varieties for optimal flavor throughout the winter. As you master these preservation techniques, you'll find they're not just about saving food for later. They're also an opportunity to expand your culinary skills, express your creativity, and take your homegrown meals to new heights. So, as you delve into the world of food preservation, embrace the opportunities for innovation that come with it.

Fermenting and pickling

If you've ever tasted the tangy crunch of a dill pickle or the complex flavors of sauerkraut, you've experienced the magic of fermentation and pickling. These age-old preservation techniques not only extend the shelf life of fresh produce but also enhance their flavor and nutritional value. They can open up a world of culinary possibilities for beginners and experienced cooks alike.

Understanding Fermentation and Pickling
Fermentation and pickling are both methods of preserving food, but they work in slightly different ways:

- Fermentation is a process where microorganisms, such as bacteria, yeast, or molds, convert sugars in food into other substances like alcohol, gases, or acids. This process can preserve food and also create unique flavors, textures, and nutritional properties.

- Pickling is a broader term that includes any process for preserving food in an acidic solution. This can be done through fermentation, as in the case of fermented pickles or sauerkraut, or by simply immersing the food in vinegar, as in the case of quick pickles.

The Benefits of Fermenting and Pickling
Fermenting and pickling come with several benefits:

1. Preservation: They extend the shelf life of fresh produce, allowing you to enjoy seasonal foods year-round.

2. Flavor: They can add complex flavors and textures to otherwise simple foods.

3. Nutrition: Fermented foods can be easier to digest and may have enhanced nutritional properties due to the action of beneficial bacteria.

Getting Started with Fermenting
Fermentation can seem intimidating, but it's actually quite simple once you understand the basics. Here are some steps to get you started:

1. Choose Your Produce: Almost any fresh vegetable can be fermented, but some popular choices include cabbage (for making sauerkraut or kimchi), cucumbers, and carrots.

2. Prepare Your Produce: Clean and chop your vegetables as desired. For fermentation, it's important to use fresh, high-quality produce for the best results.

3. Add Salt: Salt is crucial in fermentation as it inhibits harmful bacteria and allows beneficial bacteria to thrive. The amount of salt needed can vary, but a common ratio is 1-3% salt by weight of the vegetables.

4. Pack Your Jar: Pack your vegetables and salt tightly into a clean jar, leaving some space at the top. The vegetables should release enough

liquid to be submerged under the brine. If not, you can add a little water.

5. Ferment: Cover the jar loosely and let it sit at room temperature, out of direct sunlight. The fermentation time can vary from a few days to several weeks, depending on the temperature and your taste preferences.

6. Store: Once the fermentation is to your liking, cap the jar and store it in the fridge to slow down further fermentation.

Getting Started with Pickling
Pickling with vinegar is even simpler than fermenting. Here's a basic process:

1. Choose and Prepare Your Produce: Just like with fermenting, you can pickle a wide variety of vegetables.

2. Make a Pickling Solution: This usually consists of vinegar, water, and salt, and sometimes sugar. The vinegar should be of a high enough acidity (usually 5%) to preserve the vegetables.

3. Pack Your Jar: Place the vegetables in a clean jar and pour the pickling solution over them, making sure they are completely covered.

4. Seal and Refrigerate: Seal the jar and refrigerate it for at least a few hours before eating. The pickles will continue to develop flavor over time.

Safety is important when fermenting and pickling. Always use clean equipment and fresh produce, and be sure to submerge your vegetables under the brine or pickling solution to prevent mold. If you see any signs of spoilage, such as mold, an off smell, or sliminess, it's best to err on the side of caution and discard the batch.
While fermenting and pickling are often used for preserving vegetables, they can also be applied to other foods. For instance, you can ferment dairy to make yogurt or cheese, and you can pickle fruits for a tangy treat. So, don't be afraid to experiment and find your own favorite combinations!

In addition to their culinary benefits, fermenting and pickling are also a great way to reduce food waste. You can ferment or pickle leftover vegetables that might otherwise go bad. Even the brine from fermented foods or pickles can be used, for instance, as a flavorful salad dressing or marinade. Therefore, these techniques not only allow you to create delicious and nutritious foods but also contribute to a more sustainable and conscious way of cooking.

Preventing waste of surplus produce

The realization that there was an overabundance angered providence, but the plenty continued to delight people. The spirit of generosity was maintained via careful management:

Keeping the shelves in the refrigerator orderly allowed for a longer availability of the abundance, which allowed for the freshest items to be consumed first and prevented overlook age in the middle of the confusion.

The process of dehydrating food can result in increased nutrition density, convenience, sun-dried tomatoes, and the ability to readily reconstitute soups during the winter with very little work.

On the counter, sauerkraut, cultured probiotics, and lactic-fermented peppers are fermenting, helping to reduce waste while introducing helpful bacteria and facilitating digestion.

The process of freezing blanched greens that have been blended into pesto, which then serves as the base for the substitution of cooking oil engaged prolonged through winter nutrition's cooler boosting everything that is tossed.

Sharing farming's advantages in the absence of tragedy where everyone possess adequate communal strength exists is where gleanings are donated, yield estimates are overestimated, and those who are food insecure are gratefully fed.

Through trading and imaginative redistribution, the crafts that were most desired were given to the appropriate neighbors. Gazed longingly realizing that none of them wished to lessen another's fullness cooperation's surest seed planting started from inside.

Lessons learnt, reduction of excess, concentration on plenty, maintenance of the earth's generosity, a break from mindless multiplication, introspection, and feeding fleeting desires alone with wisdom's frugality: these are the things that nurture spirits in an enduring way.

The following are some further suggestions for avoiding the waste that comes from having an abundance of produce:

If you want to avoid wasting the qualities of soft fruits while they are still ripe, you may juice them or combine them into smoothies.

Produce leathers and baby food can be made by pureeing bits of fruit or vegetables into a spread or puree, respectively.

Canning or pickling vegetables with straightforward methods allows you to store them for a long time after their freshness has passed their optimum.

Assemble "imperfection bags" of defective fruits and vegetables and sell them to other people at a reduced price.

Recycle the nutrients that are lost in the process of peeling and coring fruits and vegetables by adding them to compost.

Invite the people who live nearby to a day of gleaning so that they can take what they need to eat before the harvests are lost.

Investigate the possibility of creating value-added items out of excess components, such as spicy sauces, salsas, or baked goods.

To learn about less popular ways of preservation, such as lacto-fermenting vegetables, see preservation guidelines.

Donate any extra crops by working with food banks, pantries, or meal programs to coordinate the process.

Selling or donating extras

Overflowing baskets of tomatoes, bunches of fresh herbs, or a surplus of ripe, juicy peaches can be a wonderful problem to have. However, when your garden produces more than you can consume or preserve, it's time to consider other options. Selling or donating your extras is a great way to ensure nothing goes to waste and can even bring additional benefits. Let's explore how to make the most of your surplus produce.

Selling Your Surplus
If you have a consistent surplus, selling your extra produce can be a rewarding way to offset gardening costs or even generate some income. Here's how to get started:

- Farmers' Markets: These local events are a popular venue to sell your goods. Just be sure to check the requirements as some markets only allow certified organic growers or have other stipulations.

- Roadside Stands: A classic method for selling extras, especially if you live in a rural area or on a well-traveled road. Remember to display your produce attractively and price it competitively.

- Online Marketplaces: Local online marketplaces can be a great way to reach customers in your area. Websites and apps dedicated to local food sales are becoming more prevalent.

Donating Your Surplus
If your goal is to support your community, donating your surplus produce can be incredibly rewarding.

- Food Banks and Pantries: Many food banks welcome fresh produce donations and it's a great way to help those in need. However, do call in advance to check their requirements.

- Community Kitchens: These establishments prepare meals for community members and can often use fresh ingredients.

- Schools: Some schools have programs for healthy eating and may welcome the donation of fresh fruits and vegetables.

Remember that selling or donating your surplus produce not only helps prevent waste but also allows others to enjoy the fruits of your labor. It's an opportunity to connect with your community, support local food systems, and share the joys of fresh, homegrown food. Though selling and donating excess produce are both fantastic routes to take, there's another option that blends the two: consider a "pay-what-you-can" model. This strategy is particularly effective at local farmer's markets or community events. You simply set up a stand with your surplus produce, but instead of setting firm prices, customers pay what they are able. This approach not only ensures that your produce doesn't go to waste but also makes fresh, local food more accessible to those who may not normally be able to afford it. It's a gesture that reinforces community bonds, supports inclusivity, and upholds the principle that everyone deserves access to fresh, healthy food. You may not make a large profit, but the social benefits can be substantial. So, if you find yourself with more produce than you know what to do with, try out a "pay-what-you-can" stand – you might be surprised at the positive response.

Bonus Book 1 - Getting Started with Hydroponics

Overview of hydroponic gardening methods

Exploring soilless systems availability was prompted by curiosity, which led to the uncovering of new dimensions:

The use of ebb and flow procedures, in which the roots are intermittently submerged before being allowed to drain, enables intimate monitoring. Timers are used to automate floods, which ensures that oxygenation occurs between waterings and accommodates competent novices with hectic schedules.

Deep water culture suspends plants inside mineral nutrient solutions, the levels of which are growing gradually. This eases comparable management without the need for bulky soils' parameter balancing scales, which increases complexity gradually.

The nutrient film technique continually moves water over slanted tables, avoiding substrate buildup while oxygen-rich water envelops the plant's roots. This method is extremely effective, but it requires the utmost care and technical precision, as even the smallest disturbances can have a devastating effect.

Wick systems raise pots above resting reservoirs that are kept moist by depending passively on wicks to transfer solutions. Despite this, there is a danger of separation from non-wetted roots, which is only tolerated by a small number of plants.

Flood and drain systems fill basins, which are then drained via holes in the reservoir tops, thereby preserving moist media while also simplifying the process without the use of pumping or manual watering and ensuring that essential contact is maintained. This may be easily adapted to meet any system's complexity.

Experimentation and the development of new methods favorites marrying advantages varying depending to the dynamics of different microclimates inside and outdoors, fostering the thrill of discovery while building communities via cooperative learning and wherever one's curiosity may go, abundance will follow as a patient but certain reward for those who pay attention to nature's cycles while having fun along the way.

Additional information on hydroponic growing techniques is provided below:

As a means of support, media beds make use of inert materials such as rockwool or perlite, and fertilizers are distributed in a consistent manner via lines.

Raft systems require temperature adjustment since they float plants on polystyrene disks on nutrient-rich water in pools. Raft systems are also known as hydroponic systems.

In aeroponics, roots are grown without the need of medium and are misted intermittently while suspended in air. This maximizes the supply of oxygen and nutrients.

Hybrid systems incorporate characteristics from several sources. - For instance, the NFT would go at the bottom, followed by the medium grow bed, which would provide additional support.

Choices of plants, requirements for equipment, climatic controls, fertilizer management, cleaning and maintenance are all important aspects to take into account.

Before making an investment in more complicated automated installations, start with less complicated designs such as flood-and-drain or wick systems.

Hydroponics enables year-round production in any environment, but it is necessary to carefully regulate the amounts of nutrients, pH, and temperatures in the growing medium.

Community gardens have the ability to use hydroponics and aquaponics on a wider scale via collaborative effort and the establishment of appropriate infrastructure.

Selecting an indoor or outdoor hydroponic system

Hydroponics, the technique of growing plants without soil, has gained popularity for its efficiency and versatility. Whether you're a beginner or an experienced gardener, deciding between an indoor or outdoor hydroponic system is a crucial step. Your choice will depend on several factors, including available space, climate, and the crops you wish to grow. Let's dive into the specifics of each system to help you make an informed decision.

Indoor Hydroponic Systems
Indoor hydroponic systems offer year-round growing in a controlled environment. Here's what to consider:

- Space: Indoor systems are ideal if you lack outdoor space. They can fit in a spare room, basement, or even a closet.

- Control: With an indoor system, you have complete control over temperature, lighting, and humidity, which can lead to higher yields and faster growth.

- Crops: Indoor systems are great for growing herbs, lettuce, spinach, and other small plants.

However, indoor systems require investment in grow lights and temperature control equipment, which can add to the initial cost.

Outdoor Hydroponic Systems
Outdoor systems take advantage of natural light and can allow for larger plants. Here are some key considerations:

- Climate: Outdoor systems work best in moderate climates. Extreme temperatures or precipitation can harm your plants or require costly equipment to mitigate.

- Size: If you have plenty of outdoor space, you can set up a larger system to grow more or larger plants like tomatoes or cucumbers.

- Light: Outdoor systems benefit from natural sunlight, reducing the need for artificial lights.

However, outdoor systems are exposed to pests and weather changes, which can require more attention and maintenance.

Both indoor and outdoor hydroponic systems have their advantages and challenges. Your choice will depend on your available space, desired crops, and willingness to invest in necessary equipment. While weighing the pros and cons of indoor and outdoor hydroponic systems, an often overlooked, but viable alternative is a hybrid system. Hybrid systems, also known as semi-closed systems, combine the best of both worlds. They are typically housed in greenhouses or other structures that provide some protection from the elements while still allowing for natural light penetration.
Hybrid systems offer the environmental control of indoor systems with the light utilization and potential size of outdoor systems. They can be a particularly effective solution in climates with moderate weather variability. For instance, during the warmer months, you can open doors or vents to allow natural ventilation, while in colder periods, you can close the system and use heaters to maintain an optimal growing environment. This flexibility can lead to enhanced plant growth and productivity, making it a valuable consideration for your hydroponic gardening journey.

Choosing the right hydroponic growing media

For rooted advances, sensible mediums that have been properly studied are required:
Expanded clay aggregates may sustain compressions while simultaneously holding air to a crucial level and fragmenting to the point where they might potentially pierce delicate tissues. Replacing a lost structure has a number of issues.

The use of perlite helps with drainage, prevents waterlogging and rotting, is primarily nourishing, supporting, lightweight, and easy to alter; nevertheless, abrasive touch increases the danger of dehydration and requires careful handling.

Rockwool is extensively used in professional settings, although it expands and binding chemicals are difficult to remove, and its ultimate compost ability is questioned. Rockwool excels in aeration, durability, and pH stabilization.

Coco coir charms make usage more convenient. Buffers, variations, naturally occurring coconut husk byproducts, and harmlessly decaying praised low-tech gardens may require reinforcement due to mineral leaching.

Organic media, mixes, and appeal are great for beginners since they are acquainted soils, the notion of biodegradability, and ultimately necessitate replenishing nutrients, microhard, frequent maintenance, and enjoyable challenges.

Alternatives are explored by innovation. Respecting the earth's environmental limits and providing just compensation on an annual basis those harvests, technologies, fruits, possibly future understandings that will overcome the present restrictions, amply nourish all creatures, and do so peacefully.

Additional suggestions for selecting the appropriate growth medium are as follows:

When deciding on the density and porosity of the medium, it is important to take into account both the kind of system being used (ebb and flow versus DWC) and the requirements of the plant.

To get a balance of qualities, try experimenting with other mixing medium such as perlite, clay pellets, and coconut coir.

Before committing substantial quantities to a system, it is important to conduct runoff EC and pH tests on a variety of media.

Peat and compost are examples of organic medium, both of which require more nutrients but offer additional advantages to the microbial activity.

It is important to inspect and rinse the media on a regular basis, especially expanded clay or rockwool, which can accumulate salt.

If the rockwool or clay pellets are not contaminated, they can be used again after being completely rinsed between harvests.

When properly cared for, inert choices might endure for many years, whilst biodegradable ones would need to be replaced every year.

When making your choice, be sure to take into account how sustainably the resources were sourced as well as any potential negative effects on the environment.

It is important to keep an eye on the state of the roots and make any necessary adjustments to the watering and atmosphere as the medium ages and its porosity shifts.

Maintaining optimal nutrient levels

Maintaining optimal nutrient levels is crucial to the health, growth, and yield of your plants. In traditional soil-based gardening, nutrients are provided by the soil and organic matter. However, in other forms of gardening such as hydroponics, aquaponics, or container gardening, gardeners must provide all the necessary nutrients. Understanding what nutrients your plants need and how to provide them can spell the difference between a thriving garden and a failing one.

Essential Nutrients
Plants need 16 essential nutrients to grow and produce fruit or flowers. These nutrients are divided into three categories:

- Macronutrients: Nitrogen (N), Phosphorus (P), Potassium (K), Calcium (Ca), Magnesium (Mg), and Sulfur (S).

- Micronutrients: Iron (Fe), Manganese (Mn), Boron (B), Copper (Cu), Zinc (Zn), Molybdenum (Mo), and Chlorine (Cl).
- Non-Mineral Nutrients: Hydrogen (H), Oxygen (O), and Carbon (C).

Each nutrient plays a unique role in plant growth. For instance, Nitrogen promotes leaf and stem growth, while Phosphorous is essential for root development and flowering.

Maintaining Nutrient Levels
Here are some steps to ensure your plants get the nutrients they need:

- Understand Your Plants' Needs: Different plants have different nutrient requirements. Research your specific plants to understand their nutrient needs.

- Use Quality Fertilizers: Use a balanced, high-quality fertilizer that contains all the necessary macronutrients and micronutrients.

- Monitor and Adjust: Regularly test your soil or water (in hydroponic systems) to monitor nutrient levels. Adjust your feeding regimen based on these tests.

- Watch for Deficiencies: Nutrient deficiencies often show up as specific symptoms such as yellowing leaves or stunted growth. Learn to recognize these signs to address deficiencies promptly.

- Avoid Over-fertilization: More is not always better. Over-fertilization can lead to nutrient burn or an imbalance in the nutrient solution, which can harm your plants.

While it's important to ensure your plants receive all necessary nutrients, it's equally important to remember that balance is key. Overloading your plants with nutrients can be just as detrimental as not providing enough. It's essential to find the right balance that allows your plants to thrive.

In addition to the traditional nutrients, there's another aspect that's critical for optimizing nutrient uptake in plants: the pH level. The pH level of the water or soil in which your plants are growing can significantly impact how well they can absorb the nutrients available to them. Most plants prefer a slightly acidic environment (a pH of 6 to 6.5), but some plants have different preferences. Regularly testing and adjusting the pH of your growing medium can help ensure that your plants are able to effectively absorb the nutrients they need. If you're growing in soil, you can adjust pH with lime (to raise pH) or sulfur (to lower pH). In a hydroponic setup, pH can be adjusted using solutions specifically designed for this purpose. By paying attention to pH as well as nutrient levels, you can create an ideal environment for your plants to grow and thrive.

Bonus Book 2 - Leveraging Vertical Space for Increased Yields

Benefits of vertical gardening

Being resourceful motivates one to make the most of one's limits creatively:

Walls can be used as supports for climbing plants such as tomatoes and cucumbers in order to provide an aesthetic effect. Staking Vertical providesexhibitionsthatarebountifulandthatencourageparticipationinha rvests.

Trellises positioned above beds incline bountiful beans and peas toward sunshine, allowing for more equal and prolonged ripening than would occur on level soil that is prone to shadow and wetness.

rooftops affixed to towers as access points community space, shelter in place, urban farms, suburban porches, and balconies Beginning on a smaller scale can be helpful in nourishing neighborhoods.

Planters with modular raised beds Stack multi-levels of surfaces everywhere that are edible, integrating them into living spaces indoors and outdoors, particularly in productively underutilized corners.

Canopies, green screens, privacy fences, and training mesh all come together to form a grant. Semi-privacy that is reinforced by color, texture, and beauty in the amenity.

Innovative buildings that provide refuge for poultry may become alive with vines that yield food, medicine, and herbs during the changing seasons through a process known as symbiosis.

Future researches, builds, and constructs living buildings with microclimates that are conducive to effective nesting. Join up the dots

We're Much Closer to Nature's Riches Restoring and Saving in Full Capacity Delightfully urban ghettos Urban Ghettos

The following is a list of other advantages of vertical gardening:

- Makes efficient use of space by expanding vertically rather than horizontally, hence increasing output from a constrained area.

- Increases the quality of the crop by ensuring that vines, wall, and trellis plants receive the optimum amount of sun exposure from a variety of angles.

- Can be used to create privacy screens or living walls, both of which enhance the appearance of outdoor places while still providing food.

- By maximizing the amount of solar gain that crops receive through insulated south-facing surfaces, the growth season is lengthened.

- Creates landscape designs that tastefully include food plants without sacrificing the landscape's overall visual appeal.

Rather of having to lean over elevated beds, crops may be brought to a suitable plucking height, which makes harvesting much simpler.

- Encourages the planting of many stories by stacking plants of varied heights, including climbers, vines, and rambling plants.

- Serves as aesthetic focal points or borders by showcasing decorative and espalier-trained edible plant varieties.

- Utilizes vertical habitat that is typically underused by ground-dwelling plants and animals in order to create a more biodiverse environment.

Types of vertical structures and supports

Vertical gardening, the practice of growing plants upward rather than outwards, is a fantastic way to maximize space, increase yields, and create visually appealing gardens. Using vertical structures and supports, you can transform a tiny patio or an urban balcony into a lush, productive garden. This chapter will guide you through the different types of vertical structures and supports, their benefits, and how to choose the right one for your garden.

Trellises
Trellises are one of the most common types of vertical supports used in gardening. They are typically made from wood, metal, or plastic and consist of a flat framework of latticework. Trellises are great for supporting climbing plants such as peas, beans, cucumbers, and vining flowers like morning glories or clematis.

Pergolas
Pergolas are larger structures often used as a shady walkway or relaxing sitting area in a garden. They are typically made of vertical posts or pillars that support cross-beams and a sturdy open lattice. Vining plants, especially those that produce flowers or fruit like grapes, wisteria, or climbing roses, are ideal for pergolas.

Vertical Planters
Vertical planters are containers designed to hold plants in a vertical arrangement. They can be freestanding units, wall-mounted, or hung from ceilings. Vertical planters are excellent for growing a variety of small plants, including herbs, strawberries, or ornamental flowers, and are perfect for small spaces like balconies or patios.

Obelisks and Towers
Obelisks and towers are freestanding structures that provide a lot of vertical space and can serve as a stunning focal point in your garden. They are excellent for supporting climbing flowers, tomatoes, or pole beans.

Espaliers
An espalier is a plant that is trained to grow flat against a wall, fence, or trellis. While traditionally used for fruit trees like apples or pears, espaliers can be used for a variety of plants. This method requires more effort in training and pruning, but the result can be a beautiful and productive wall of plants.

When choosing the right structure or support for your garden, consider the type of plants you want to grow, the space available, and the aesthetic you want to achieve. It's also essential to ensure the structure is sturdy enough to support the full weight of the plants when they are mature and laden with fruit.

Vertical gardening is not just limited to outdoor gardens. Indoor gardeners can also benefit from vertical structures, particularly when space is limited. Hanging baskets, wall-mounted planters, or even a bookshelf can provide valuable vertical growing space for houseplants, herbs, or salad greens.

However, when planning an indoor vertical garden, it's important to consider the light requirements of the plants you want to grow. All plants need light to photosynthesize and grow, but the amount of light required can vary widely between different plant species. Some plants, such as many herbs and succulents, need lots of bright light, while others, like ferns and ivies, can thrive in lower light conditions. If you're growing plants indoors, make sure your vertical garden is situated near a window that gets adequate sunlight, or consider investing in grow lights to ensure your plants get the light they need. With a bit of planning and creativity, you can create a vertical garden that is both functional and beautiful, regardless of the size of your space.

Training vining crops to climb vertically

Play is the path to mastery, as it allows vines to reward those that explore freely:

Peas that are slid between the canes excite the curled tendrils that are grabbing, demonstrating that the frames are supportive and stimulating profuse production prototropically.

Cucumbers that are trained to coil themselves around strings that are supported by robust poles progressively extend the length of the branches that yield fruit in a horizontal direction, increasing their exposure while minimizing the amount of needless soil contact and promoting charity.

Melons were massaged along mulched rows, which caused them to sprout adventurous laterals, hopefully exploring ornamented trellises, and soon moored productively. This was done to prevent sprawling melons from succumbing to infections, which would weaken them further. In addition, nourished upright melons were kindly sharing the delights of plentitude.

Squash that has been cultivated on anchored meshes tends to flourish exuberantly, beautifying entryways joyfully declaring bountiful household's hands conjuredseasonally uniting communities and occasionally caring for those who are left over.

Tomatoes crept cautiously up the vertical cages for guidance before eventually becoming secure and independent. Climbing magnificently painted balconies and railings that were filled with readily available and easily picked blooms in surroundings that were urban or country in appearance,

Experimentation ever refines tactics, inviting the exuberance of nature while remaining within prudent limitations, and community sharing is encouraged. Lessons learnt through patient compassion and discovery's ever-renewing delight are passed down from generation to generation.

The following are some more suggestions for vertically training vine-type crops:

Rather of trying to train mature sprawlers to stand up straight, begin fresh plants in close proximity to supports to stimulate early climbing.

First, secure or direct the growth of the main stems, and then go on to the side shoots, in order to keep the leaves and fruits distributed evenly.

- Select the sort of support that is most appropriate for the crop, such as thin strings or nets for cucumbers and stronger cages or fences for tomatoes with big fruit loads.

It is important to do periodic lateral pruning in order to keep the canopy open and allow for easy access to harvest the fruit.

- To prevent the supports from toppling over under the weight of the crop load, ensure that they are securely fastened in soil that drains effectively.

Instead of growing lengthy horizontal rows, staking or caging each individual plant is a preferable strategy for disease and insect control.

Experiment with different espalier techniques to create an aesthetic effect by fanning out plants against fences or other structures.

- It is important to take into consideration both indeterminate and determinate kinds that are suitable for vertical growth habits.

- Pay attention to the outcomes in order to perfect your preferred positioning, tying methods, and supports for the upcoming growing season.

Optimizing sunlight for vertical crops

Harnessing the power of the sun, the ultimate source of energy for all life on Earth, is vital for successful vertical gardening. Sunlight plays a crucial role in photosynthesis, the process by which plants convert light energy into chemical energy to fuel their growth. This chapter will guide you through effective strategies to optimize sunlight for your vertical crops, ensuring bountiful yields and healthy growth.

Understanding Sun Exposure
Before we delve into the strategies, it's essential to understand the concept of sun exposure. Sun exposure is generally categorized into three types:

- Full sun: At least six hours of direct sunlight each day. Vegetables and flowering plants usually require full sunlight.
- Partial sun/shade: Three to six hours of sunlight per day, preferably in the morning or early afternoon. Many herbs and leafy vegetables, like lettuce and spinach, do well in partial sun.

- Full shade: Less than three hours of direct sunlight each day. A few plants like ferns and some types of hostas can tolerate these conditions.

Positioning Vertical Structures for Optimal Sunlight
Positioning your vertical garden to maximize sun exposure is the first step in optimizing sunlight. Here are a few tips:

- Orientation matters: In the Northern Hemisphere, south-facing gardens receive the most sunlight. If possible, position your vertical garden facing south.

- Consider the Sun's Path: Remember, the sun's path changes with the seasons. The sun is lower in the sky in winter and higher in the summer. Ensure your vertical structure doesn't shade other parts of your garden.

- Avoid Shady Areas: Avoid placing your vertical garden near taller structures or trees that could cast a shadow over your garden for significant parts of the day.

Choosing the Right Crops
Choosing the right crops for your vertical garden is as crucial as positioning. Some plants naturally do better in certain light conditions:

- Full Sun Plants: Tomatoes, cucumbers, squash, and most flowering plants need full sun to produce a good yield.

- Partial Sun/Shade Plants: Leafy greens, like lettuce and spinach, herbs like parsley and mint, and some fruits like strawberries, can tolerate less sun.

Using Reflective Materials
Reflective materials can be used to increase the amount of light that reaches your plants. These materials reflect sunlight onto the leaves of your plants, which can be particularly useful for plants situated lower on a vertical structure. Reflective mulches or white plastic can

be used on the ground, or you can use lighter colors for walls and fences to help reflect sunlight.

Pruning for Sunlight Optimization
Regularly pruning your plants helps ensure that sunlight can reach all parts of your plants. Pruning allows better air circulation and light penetration, reducing the risk of disease while encouraging more robust growth.

Vertical gardening opens up a new dimension of possibilities for home gardeners, urban farmers, and anyone limited by space. While it presents unique challenges, such as ensuring adequate sunlight, these can be overcome with strategic planning and creative solutions. A less traditional method to optimize sunlight for your vertical crops involves utilizing artificial light sources. While natural sunlight is the best and most cost-effective source of light for plants, there are situations where it may not be sufficient. For example, in densely built urban environments, nearby buildings may block sunlight for much of the day. In such cases, or when growing plants indoors, artificial light sources such as grow lights can be a beneficial supplement. Grow lights come in various types, including fluorescent bulbs, high-intensity discharge lamps, and light-emitting diodes (LEDs). Each type of light has its pros and cons, and the best choice depends on factors like the types of plants you're growing, your budget, and the size of your growing area. While using artificial light adds an extra layer of complexity to vertical gardening, it also allows for greater control over the growing environment, potentially leading to even more abundant and healthy crops.

Bonus Book 3 - Embracing Permaculture Principles for Sustainable Gardening

Introduction to Permaculture

Simply by studying how nature was designed, interdependence serves as an inspiration for the abundance of sustainable living:

Permaculture recognizes sustainability as resulting from different synergies rather than monocultures. It looks at naturally occurring systems as symbiotically sustaining one another in a cyclical manner without producing waste. When relationships are prioritized above resources, yields may be maximized while depleted land can be restored. revealing concealed wealth that is attainable via attentive practice that resembles The example of rich output provided by forest ecosystems while only requiring minimum care once established aesthetically efficient perpetual husbandry's secrets were discovered far sooner in antiquity and incorporated than laboriously learned piecemeal sustainability's basis. Therefore, the answer resides not just in production but also in relationships. Support in sustaining life The result of this is the spontaneous emergence of cooperatively circulated abundance.

Through the careful incorporation of planted Zones Imitating the evolutionary processes of nature as a form of strategy Mutually beneficial relationships develop over time. Providing assistance to the whole Developing productive spaces or nooks This imagined terrain, which is home to a wide variety of flora and fauna, contains wealth that is equally available to everyone vital Now and forever, always renewing life, all participants freely contributing, constantly developing this approach. The promise of restoring Harmony, equilibrium inhabitants of armangites Where healing comes from food and wellbeing flows freely free-flowing and soaring in song

The following is a list of some more permaculture methods and principles:
- Utilizing components that serve several purposes and meet a variety of requirements (for example, fruit trees that fix nitrogen);

- Zoning that is more concerned with the frequency of usage than with aesthetics alone in order to maximize efficiency

- Increasing both biodiversity and the area's capacity for resilience through the use of edges and interwoven components

- Recognizing animals of all species as important contributors to the overall system

- Stacking items in both the vertical and horizontal planes in order to get the most out of each space

- Completing nutrient cycles through practices such as composting and mulching in order to increase the fertility of the soil over time

- Creating productive, linked landscapes by emulating the patterns that are seen in nature

- Examining the effects of the long term through the prism of renewability and sustaining yields

- Facilitating the process of natural succession in order to create low-intervention, productive ecosystems

- Permaculture design and ethics center on the need of placing a high value on people and community as key assets.

- Placing more of an emphasis on regional variations and traditional wisdom as opposed to universal standards

Designing a Permaculture Garden Here

Permaculture, a portmanteau of "permanent culture," is an agricultural system that works with, rather than against, nature. It's a holistic approach that strives to create a balanced ecosystem, enriching the soil, conserving water, and promoting biodiversity. In this chapter, we'll explore the key principles of permaculture and how to design a permaculture garden in your backyard.

Understanding Permaculture Principles
Permaculture embraces a set of core principles that guide its design and implementation. Here are the key ones:

- Observe and Interact: Each site is unique. Spend time observing your garden's conditions, like sunlight, soil, and local wildlife, to understand how to work with these elements rather than battling against them.

- Capture and Store Energy: This principle encourages the storage of surplus resources. For example, you can capture rainwater for irrigation or compost kitchen waste to enrich your soil.

- Obtain a Yield: Ensure your garden is productive. This doesn't only mean growing food but can also include growing medicinal herbs or plants that attract beneficial insects.

- Apply Self-Regulation and Accept Feedback: Learn from your successes and failures and make necessary adjustments.

- Use and Value Renewables: Make the most of renewable resources, such as wind and sun, rather than relying on non-renewable resources.

Steps to Design a Permaculture Garden
Now that we have an understanding of the principles, let's move on to the steps involved in designing a permaculture garden.

Step 1: Observe and Assess Your Site
Spend time observing your potential garden site throughout the year. Notice where the sun rises and sets, where water collects, which areas are windy, and the quality of your soil. Observing your site will inform your design decisions.

Step 2: Design for Your Site
Based on your observations, start to sketch a plan for your garden. Remember to work with your site, not against it. For example, place water-loving plants in low-lying areas that collect water, and plant windbreaks in windy areas.

Step 3: Choose the Right Plants
Choose a mix of plants that work together to create a balanced ecosystem. This might include food crops, herbs, flowers to attract pollinators, and plants that enrich the soil, such as legumes.

Step 4: Implement Your Design
Once you're happy with your design, it's time to get to work. Start small and expand gradually. This will give you a chance to learn and make adjustments as necessary.

Step 5: Observe and Tweak
Once your garden is established, continue observing and tweaking. A permaculture garden is a living system that will change and grow over time.

Permaculture not only provides a sustainable way to garden but also creates a beautiful, productive outdoor space that benefits local wildlife. It's a rewarding practice that can transform your garden into a vibrant, resilient ecosystem.

In addition to the principles and design steps outlined above, it's also worth mentioning the concept of "zones" in permaculture design. Zones help in organizing your garden based on the frequency of human use and plant or animal needs. The house, or home center, is referred to as Zone 0, with other zones numbered sequentially based on how often you visit them. Zone 1, which is the area immediately surrounding the house, typically includes plants that need frequent attention, such as herbs and salad vegetables. Further zones have lesser interaction and might include larger fruit trees, compost bins, and even wild areas for attracting biodiversity. Designing with zones can make your garden more efficient and easier to manage, saving time and energy while also meeting the needs of different plants and animals.

Permaculture Techniques for Year-Round Gardening

Year-round gardening is a rewarding venture that ensures a continuous supply of fresh produce no matter the season. Through the application of permaculture techniques, this dream can become a reality. Permaculture, which blends science and art, provides a guide on how to create resilient and sustainable gardens. Let's delve into how these techniques can facilitate year-round gardening.

Understanding Permaculture and Seasons
Before we delve into the techniques, it's important to understand how permaculture intersects with the changing seasons. Permaculture thrives on diversity and recognizes that each season brings its unique set of conditions. By working with these natural changes, you can create a garden that produces food throughout the year.

Planting Perennials
Perennials are plants that live for more than two years, and they are a cornerstone of permaculture gardening. Unlike annuals that need to be replanted each year, perennials keep coming back. This not only saves time and energy but also helps to create soil stability and increase biodiversity. Examples of perennials include asparagus, rhubarb, many types of berries, and numerous herbs like rosemary and thyme.

Succession Planting
Succession planting involves growing one crop immediately after another. This technique maximizes the use of garden space and ensures a continuous harvest. For instance, after harvesting spring peas, you can plant heat-loving peppers in the same space for summer, followed by cool-season crops like kale for the fall.

Using Greenhouses and Cold Frames
Greenhouses and cold frames can extend the growing season by providing plants with a protected growing environment. This allows you to start seeds early in the spring and keep harvesting well into the fall and winter. Both structures work by trapping heat from the sun and reducing wind chill.

Incorporating Animals
Animals can play a pivotal role in a permaculture garden and can contribute to year-round productivity. Chickens, for example, can provide eggs almost year-round. They also help with pest control and produce manure that enriches the soil. Bees are excellent pollinators,

and they produce honey, while worms can be used to break down kitchen scraps and produce nutrient-rich compost.

Creating Microclimates
Microclimates are small areas within your garden that have slightly different conditions than the surrounding area. These can be created intentionally to extend the growing season. For instance, a wall that receives lots of sun can radiate heat and create a warm microclimate where you can grow plants that typically wouldn't survive in your region.

Permaculture techniques offer a bounty of benefits, from creating sustainable and resilient landscapes to providing a year-round supply of fresh produce. As a gardener, the shift to permaculture may demand learning new skills and changing perspectives, but the rewards are well worth it.
To further enhance the productivity of your permaculture garden, consider incorporating the principle of stacking. This involves making use of vertical space in the garden, which is often underutilized in traditional gardening systems. By growing plants at different heights, you can cultivate a more diverse array of crops in the same space. For example, tall trees might form the canopy layer, under which lower-growing fruit trees thrive. Beneath these, you might grow shade-tolerant herbs and vegetables. This not only maximizes space but also mimics natural ecosystems, leading to healthier and more productive gardens. A well-designed stacking system can provide food and other resources at all times of the year, further supporting the goal of year-round gardening.

Made in the USA
Las Vegas, NV
25 October 2023

79638021R00063